The World of
Whistler

TIME
LIFE
BOOKS
®

HUMAN BEHAVIOR

THE ART OF SEWING

THE OLD WEST

THE EMERGENCE OF MAN

THE AMERICAN WILDERNESS

THE TIME-LIFE ENCYCLOPEDIA OF GARDENING

LIFE LIBRARY OF PHOTOGRAPHY

THIS FABULOUS CENTURY

FOODS OF THE WORLD

TIME-LIFE LIBRARY OF AMERICA

TIME-LIFE LIBRARY OF ART

GREAT AGES OF MAN

LIFE SCIENCE LIBRARY

THE LIFE HISTORY OF THE UNITED STATES

TIME READING PROGRAM

LIFE NATURE LIBRARY

LIFE WORLD LIBRARY

FAMILY LIBRARY:

   THE TIME-LIFE BOOK OF THE FAMILY CAR

   THE TIME-LIFE FAMILY LEGAL GUIDE

   THE TIME-LIFE BOOK OF FAMILY FINANCE

TIME-LIFE LIBRARY OF ART

The World of Whistler

1834-1903

by Tom Prideaux
and
the Editors of TIME-LIFE BOOKS

TIME-LIFE BOOKS, New York

About the Author

After more than 25 years as an editor and drama critic for LIFE, Tom Prideaux retired from that magazine in 1970 to become a full-time freelance writer. He came by his interest in Whistler while writing *The World of Delacroix* for the TIME-LIFE Library of Art. Mr. Prideaux is also the author, with Josephine Mayer, of *Never to Die*, a book on ancient Egypt.

The Consulting Editor

H. W. Janson is Professor of Fine Arts at New York University, New York City, where he is also Chairman of the Department of Fine Arts at Washington Square College. Among his many publications are *History of Art* and *The Sculpture of Donatello.*

The Consultant for This Book

Theodore Reff is Professor of Art History at Columbia University, and has also taught at The John Hopkins University and Pennsylvania State University. A former Fellow of the Institute for Advanced Study and of the John Simon Guggenheim Memorial Foundation, Dr. Reff has edited the letters of Toulouse-Lautrec, is now editing the notebooks of Degas, and is the author of numerous publications on 19th and 20th Century art.

On the Slipcase

This detail from Whistler's *Nocturne in Blue and Gold: Old Battersea Bridge* shows the elegant simplicity and subtle tonal harmony characteristic of the artist. Behind the old wooden bridge in the moonlight, the golden sparks of falling fireworks add a touch of warmth to the otherwise cool coloration. The complete painting is reproduced on page 135.

End Papers

Front: Drawing, painting and etching the Thames was a favorite occupation of Whistler. This etching, done in the 1870s, is of London's Old Putney Bridge. The artist's familiar butterfly emblem is at lower right center. *Back:* The light and color of Venice served Whistler as a profound inspiration. This is a view of the Riva degli Schiavoni near the Piazza San Marco, done about 1880.

The following individuals and departments of Time Inc. helped to produce this book: photographer, Carlo Bavagnoli; Editorial Production, Norman Airey; Library, Benjamin Lightman; Picture Collection, Doris O'Neil; Photographic Laboratory, George Karas; TIME-LIFE News Service, Murray J. Gart; Correspondents Maria Vincenza Aloisi (Paris), Martha Bucknell and Phyllis Wise (Washington, D.C.), Nat Carnes (San Juan), Margot Hapgood and Rosemary Young (London), Serrell Hillman (Toronto) and Ann Natanson (Rome).

Contents

I	A Yankee-Doodle Dandy	11
II	American on the Thames	37
III	Brotherhood of Radicals	61
IV	Whistler's Mother	77
V	Triumph and Turmoil	101
VI	A Scandalous Trial	121
VII	Veneration in Venice	141
VIII	"Art for Art's Sake"	167

Chronology of Artists: 186
Bibliography: 187
Credits and Acknowledgments: 188
Index: 189

Whistler's engaging arrogance is unmistakable in
this multiple portrait etching made in the 1880s
by Mortimer Menpes.

Portrait of
the Artist

At 22, in Paris studying art, Whistler was caught napping in this pencil sketch by fellow student Edward Poynter.

In Thomas Way's bold lithograph, Whistler's white forelock stands out like a proud feather in a cavalier's hat.

It was the peculiar fate of James McNeill Whistler to be his own rival for public attention. People who were exposed to his bursting vitality and wit were often more struck by his personality and appearance than by his art. Small, muscular and handsome, he was called "the pocket Apollo" in his youth. All through his life both his friends and his enemies made pictures of him, and caricaturists could

scarcely resist him. For there was something undeniably pictorial in his impish grins, his scowls, his elegant posturings and his famous sartorial trademarks: jaunty hats, a long cane, a wickedly mobile monocle and the lock of white hair that waved like a defiant little plume. Even in late Victorian England, when the cult of eccentricity reached a peak, Whistler had no trouble holding the spotlight.

7

From memory, Max Beerbohm drew the bellicose but dapper artist as he had appeared at a trial in 1897.

The noted caricaturist Leslie Ward, alias "Spy," satirized Whistler's dandified dress and mannerisms in 1878.

Whistler's flamboyance was in contrast with the reticence and sensitivity of his art: his colors were as muted as his voice was loud. Possibly his uninhibited behavior was a stratagem to get his art noticed. It may also have reflected the fact that he was American-born but living as an expatriate in Europe: his determined assertiveness may have masked feelings of being not truly at home. But a deeper motive for Whistler's comportment can be found in his conception of the artist's role in society. Art, he insisted, must be aloof, free from function. In contrast to the belief prevalent in his day that art should be edifying and morally uplifting, Whistler's cry was "Art for Art's sake." Artists, he argued, should be responsible to nothing but art, with beauty their only master.

With this credo to live by, a credo that was to liberate art from the excesses of 19th Century

Grinning with malicious pleasure, Whistler was sketched at a London club by Edward Tennyson Reed.

sentimentality and open the way for the abstract art of the 20th Century, it is understandable that Whistler dressed and acted the way he did. He carried many a chip on his shoulder against the pomp and piety of Victorian society and he wore his chips like epaulets. They were part of his uniform, along with his sassy white lock and beribboned boots. As an apostle of artistic freedom, it was his duty to make a spectacle of himself.

Inspired by Whistler's devilry, Aubrey Beardsley drew this fanciful illustration of Pan in a parlor for an 1890s novel, *The Dancing Faun.*

I

A Yankee-Doodle Dandy

James McNeill Whistler found classifications as galling as a strait-jacket, and escaped them whenever he could. Although he was born in Lowell, Massachusetts, on one occasion he claimed Baltimore as his birthplace and on another St. Petersburg, Russia, as if any free-spirited man had a right to change his origins any time he pleased. Although he lived mostly in England, he felt as little committed to it as to America.

Both in his art and in his private affairs he similarly refused to be stereotyped. After his student apprenticeship in 19th Century Paris, he veered toward Realism, then toward the poetic idealism of the Pre-Raphaelites and next toward Impressionism. Yet in the end he settled for his own original arrangements of poetry and hard fact. He was equally free-ranging in his friends, picking them from dock hands as well as from "swells," as he called them. He did not marry until he was 54. But with two devoted women serving him, successively for 30 years, as models, mistresses, peacemakers and housekeepers, he achieved a quasi-marital status that suited him well.

Without realizing it, Whistler did fail in one major respect to elude classification. He was peculiarly, and sometimes painfully, an American. He hungered for success. He craved approval, applause. He was a tireless, even tiresome, joker. No wild West desperado was a quicker draw with his gun than Whistler was with his wit. He used it both as a weapon and as a shield to hide his hurts.

He was a man of polish and charm, but he also had streaks of un-tamed defiance. When his wits failed, he used his fists—even though he stood only five feet four inches tall. In the seriocomic boasting that came to be his personal style was a dash of pioneer braggadocio that calls to mind America's Paul Bunyans and John Henrys, crowing over the prodigious feats they could perform. Shouting his famous "ha-ha" to proclaim his contempt or enthusiasm, Whistler was reacting like Mike Fink, the legendary Mississippi boatman who hooted that he was a ring-tailed screamer as he danced on an alligator's back—except that for Whistler the alligator was usually Britain's stuffy Royal Academy of Art. Beneath his boasting, however, was often a chilly self-doubt, perhaps a result of the rootlessness that comes of being born in a new country, then transplanted to an old one.

Outwardly Whistler was a European dandy, sporting rakish straw hats and yellow gloves. But he might as well have been a cowboy glorying in a silver-chased saddle and fancy boots, a kind of Yankee-Doodle dandy. In his showmanship and humor, and in his scorn for fake gentility, he had something in common with another complex American, Mark Twain, who was born a year after him. Both of them, incidentally, loved rivers and white suits.

Whistler has never been widely recognized as the native product that he is. In part this is because of the many years he spent in Europe (he never returned to the United States after he left in 1855, at the age of 21) and in part because of the unexpected delicacy of his art. And then—who needs to be told?—there is his mother. The freakish success of his quiet portrait of her, so blatantly exploited in Mother's Day ads and so long displayed on parlor walls as a major American icon, has tended to bury the man's identity in his mother's ubiquity.

In the annals of art, Whistler might be likened to a weather vane; he showed which way the wind was blowing and how it was shifting. But so powerful was his personality, so personal his genius, that at times the weather vane seemed to be self-propelled, spinning of its own volition. His strongest conviction was that art existed for and of itself, and should not attempt simply to duplicate nature, nor try to tell stories and convey moral lessons. This belief in "Art for Art's Sake" has, of course, been shared by many another artist, and in some cases has given rise to a shallow estheticism accompanied by fits of limp posturing. But Whistler practiced his doctrine with an almost Puritan rigor that kept him pugnaciously embroiled in the world around him.

As a corollary to this credo, he increasingly tended toward abstract art, a prophet well ahead of his time. This predilection appeared early in his career when he took up etching, a field in which he was destined to become one of the great practitioners. In this difficult medium Whistler proved a master of omission, so refining his skill that what was left out became as important as what was left in. He knew how to make a few lines convey the essential movement of a body, and he knew how to make an unfilled space convey mood and atmosphere. Inevitably he applied these talents to his painting.

To emphasize his homage to abstract principles, Whistler took to calling his portraits Arrangements and Harmonies, as if sitters' names were inconsequential; the work that every school child knows as *Whistler's Mother* was titled by him *Arrangement in Grey and Black*. His swing toward abstraction became even more pronounced in his controversial bluish night scenes, which he called Nocturnes. These scenes, with their subtle merging of tone and form, may well have influenced the young Picasso in his Blue Period.

Indeed, Whistler's revolt against realism and his turn toward poetry and abstraction presaged many later tendencies in art. Yet it would appear that more than a few viewers today are put off by his work,

Whistler was born in July 1834, in this colonial-style clapboard house in Lowell, Massachusetts, named after Francis Cabot Lowell, a pioneer in American cotton manufacturing. Lowell devised a power loom and made the town the textile capital of the world. Whistler's father directed machine shops for the Proprietors of Locks and Canals, an agency that provided waterpower for the mills of Lowell.

either by its more rarefied aspects or by his quite blameless mother. If that be the case, they are missing a key figure in the battle of modern art—and also a marvelously entertaining and revealing specimen of American character.

The precise mix of genes and environment that produced James McNeill Whistler eludes analysis—as he would have wished. It is nonetheless tempting to suggest that he inherited his jocularity from Dr. Daniel Whistler, who lived in 17th Century England and was a suppertime crony of two noted diarists, Samuel Pepys and John Evelyn; as Evelyn described him, the doctor was "the most facetious man in nature." It is also tempting to ascribe the particular affinity the artist came to feel for the Thames River to ancestors who rest in a Thames valley churchyard, and to imagine that his disdain for vital statistics stemmed from one Hugh Whistler, whose brass tomb plate reports, plain as day, that he died in 1675, "being aged 216 years."

As for more immediate forebears, the American Whistlers were descended from an Irish branch of the family planted in the United States by John Whistler, the artist's grandfather. In his youth in the 1770s John enlisted in the British Army and was shipped overseas just in time to surrender to the Americans at Saratoga. He returned to England, eloped with a baronet's daughter and sailed right back to America. Soon he enlisted in the American Army, moving his wife and ever-expanding brood—eventually there were 15 sons and daughters—from post to post in Michigan, Indiana, Kentucky and Missouri. The Whistlers got around.

Of all the children, George Washington Whistler, the artist's father, was the most outstanding. In 1814, when he was 14, he was admitted to West Point, where he was warmly admired as a festive fellow who played the flute, headed his drawing class and painted on his own. (A story goes that he jumped the gun on his future son by executing a small portrait of *his* mother, the first and original *Whistler's Mother*.)

More important, George acquired both a career and a wife at West Point. He not only was trained as an engineer—then as now the Academy's specialty—but successfully wooed the belle of West Point, Mary Swift, daughter of the Academy's surgeon. One of his Army assignments after graduation was to take charge of a surveying outfit that established boundary lines between the United States and Canada. This rugged feat in the northern wilds so impressed his brother-in-law, a consulting engineer for various private enterprises, that he persuaded George to resign his commission—by now he was a major—for a more fertile field. America was in the throes of rising railroad fever, and Major Whistler became a railroad builder in association with an Academy classmate, William McNeill.

Like the new railroad tracks, the major's activities were destined to be far flung. Numerous companies, including the Baltimore & Ohio and the Paterson and Hudson River lines, employed his services, and he also journeyed to London to confer with British engineers about their latest locomotive models. He was often absent from home, and his return was always a joyous event. Evenings would be devoted to

Photographed shortly before she died at 74, Whistler's mother had by then been widowed for about 31 years. Her husband, George Washington Whistler *(below)*, died when he was 49. Since his engineering career often kept him away from home, Anna raised her son Jimmy almost singlehandedly, and exerted a strong influence on the artist.

flute playing and singing—usually Scotch or Irish ballads, both comic and tearful—and family friends would join in. One was Anna McNeill, a sister of Whistler's business associate; she became such a fixture in the household that the Whistler children, George and Deborah, thought of her as an aunt. She became their stepmother in 1831 when Mary Whistler died of a protracted illness. After their marriage, Anna confessed to her journal that she idolized her husband. It was she who was fated to be—second only to the Virgin Mary—the world's most pictured mother.

The son who was to memorialize her was born on July 11, 1834, in Lowell, a river town north of Boston, where George Whistler was then serving as supervising engineer in charge of a locomotive works. The baby was christened James Abbott Whistler; he added McNeill to his name later. The wandering that was to mark his life began when he was three. The family moved to Stonington, Connecticut, where Major Whistler supervised the building of a railroad from Stonington to Providence, Rhode Island. Since his wife was a sister of a leading Stonington matron, Mrs. George Palmer, the Whistlers were especially welcome in their new town, one of the loveliest in New England, with prim white houses and elm-lined streets. The major had a carriage constructed on train wheels, and on Sundays it was pulled by horses along the new track to Westerly, Rhode Island, so that the family could attend church—a bit of joy riding that must have thrilled little Jimmy and gratified Mrs. Whistler, since its goal was holy.

But more distant adventures were in store. In the summer of 1842 Major Whistler accepted an invitation from Czar Nicholas I of Russia to supervise the building of a 420-mile railroad from Moscow to St. Petersburg. The major arranged that his family follow a year later. Accordingly, in August 1843 Mrs. Whistler and her flock of five—her two stepchildren, Jimmy and his two younger brothers—sailed from Boston. A stopover at Preston, in northern England, proved a memorable event. Mrs. Whistler had two half sisters living there, Alicia and Eliza, her father's children by an earlier marriage. (Big families, early deaths and second marriages produced a tangle of relationships.) These English relatives had close friends who were members of the Royal Academy in London, and for the first time in his life nine-year-old Jimmy heard lively, informal talk about the arts.

The long-awaited reunion with Major Whistler in Russia was saddened by the death of the baby of the family, Charles, who fell fatally ill of an undiagnosed disease on the last lap of the voyage. Also missing was the oldest son, George, who had returned to America to follow in his father's footsteps by taking up a career as an engineer. Mrs. Whistler was both frightened and awed by the glistening splendor of St. Petersburg, with its overtones of Oriental exoticism. Still, aware that the family's sojourn in the Russian capital was bound to be remarkable, she resolved to chronicle it faithfully in her daily journal. The Czar might have been shockingly cruel to his subjects but he was very generous to the Whistlers. He provided them with a staff of Russian servants and luxurious quarters overlooking the river Neva. Mrs.

This miniature of Whistler and his brother Willie *(seated)* was painted in Europe in the mid-1840s. The younger by two years, Willie was a placid child who caused his mother little worry. His main problem at the time was the severe homesickness that afflicted him in Russia, where the boys went to boarding school; he was invariably reduced to blubbering every Sunday night when the weekend with his family ended and the time came to return to school.

ПѢСНЯ.

A Russian cartoon of the 1850s shows a group of peasants and gentlefolk in front of a depot on the outskirts of Moscow, hailing the new railroad Whistler's father built to link that city with St. Petersburg. The line opened in 1851 amid great formality. No one was allowed to wear a hat inside the station. Burdened with bags in one hand, tickets in the other, and hats in their teeth, passengers could only bob their heads in mute greeting if they happened to meet a friend. All train personnel were required to wear military uniforms; as the conductors collected fares, sabers dangled at their sides.

Whistler was upset by the occasional drunkenness of the servants and by their effusions of gratitude; they had a tendency to drop to the floor and kiss the hem of her skirt. Like many an American living abroad, she did her best to Americanize her home, observing holidays and religious customs and plying her brood with favorite American dishes such as buckwheat cakes, for which her artist son evinced a patriotic passion throughout the rest of his life. Distrustful of the Russian ways of handling milk, the Whistlers bought and stabled their own cow in an adjacent courtyard.

While his mother worried about the family's health, Jimmy adjusted nimbly to his new life. He hero-worshiped his Swedish tutor, learned fluent French, the language preferred by the Russian gentry, and took it upon himself more and more during his father's absences on railroad building to cheer up his mother with his jokes and high spirits. It was in these Russian years that he grew aware of himself as a singular person with singular powers to charm and persuade.

There was nothing self-serving in this—at least not at this early stage of Whistler's life. His gaiety was therapeutic to others, and he felt that it was his role to keep things lively. To his mother, fresh from tidy Stonington, St. Petersburg presented an unnerving contrast. How remote—farther even than the more than 5,000 miles that separated them—was the slim little steeple of the Episcopal church on Merrimack Street from the golden bulbous domes of the Cathedral of St. Nicholas on Kommunarov Square. If Anna Whistler felt at times that she was in danger of ambush by hostile forces, it was most likely to be Jimmy who made her see the funny side of things. It was he who cracked the façade of her somber, rather horselike face until it broke gratefully into a smile.

In her journal for May 30, 1846, she wrote of a night when St. Petersburg was aglow with fireworks, flowers and parades, celebrating the Czarina Alexandra's return from a trip away from the capital. At

These impressions of Russian soldiers
are the earliest surviving sketches by
Whistler, who made them from memory
in his middle teens after returning to
America from Russia. He was fascinated
by the showy army of Czar Nicholas I,
which included not only the dragoons
pictured here with their glittering
helmets and shiny leather boots, but also
hard-riding Cossacks and ferocious
tribesmen from remote provinces who
wore silver-trimmed coats and
brandished bows and arrows.

10:30 Jimmy begged her to let him escort her "just to take a peep."
She yielded, and soon they were in a jam of jostling crowds as the Czarina's retinue approached. "I was terrified," Mrs. Whistler noted, "lest
the poles of their carriage should run into our backs, or that some horses might take fright or bite us, we were so close, but [Jimmy] laughed
heartily and aloud at my timidity. He behaved like a man. With one
arm he guarded me, and with the other kept the animals at a proper distance; and, I must confess, brilliant as the spectacle was, *my* great pleasure was derived from the conduct of my dear and manly boy."

Adored by his mother, looked up to by his younger brother, William, and admired by his half sister, Deborah, who was sure he was a
genius, Jimmy Whistler was growing up to be a show-off. But mixed
with his self-assurance was gallantry, and an assumption that if a situation had to be mastered he was the one to master it. He was developing in other ways as well. He had taken to sketching members of
the family, and his progress as an artist was furthered when a noted
visitor to St. Petersburg, the painter Sir William Allen, was invited to
dine at the Whistlers'.

A member of the Scottish Royal Academy, Sir William had a commission from the Czar to execute a large work showing his formidable
predecessor, Peter the Great, teaching his peasants to build ships. The
painter's talk about his epic canvas entranced Jimmy, and after he
had been sent to bed his mother showed Sir William some of her son's
drawings, which included an astute and lively portrait of his owlish
Aunt Alicia. Sir William's verdict was "uncommon genius," and he
urged that Jimmy be sent to the Imperial Academy of Fine Arts, which
was housed in an imposing building on an island in the river Neva.

The advice was promptly heeded, and Jimmy began to attend the Academy, learning to draw in the traditional manner—from plaster casts of classical works, rather than from life. As an American and the youngest boy in his class he proved to be a center of interest and proud of it. But he also worked very hard, and he was no more shy of his august surroundings—the Academy was one of the Czar's pet enterprises and one of the most prestigious schools in Russia—than he was of the Czarina's horses.

In what was to become a lifelong habit, Whistler learned more about art outside his classroom than in. His parents treated him often to the extensive collections of the various imperial galleries and to the Hermitage in St. Petersburg, one of the world's great museums, where he formed a lasting admiration for the cool orderliness of Flemish painting. During one of his fairly frequent attacks of rheumatic fever, which kept him painfully in bed with mustard plasters, his adoring Deborah sought about for some means to amuse him, and borrowed from a friend an enormous folio of William Hogarth's engravings. Jimmy feasted his young eyes on *Gin Lane* and *Marriage à la Mode*, loving the rowdy scenes of loose living, and declared to Mrs. Whistler: "If I had not been ill, Mother, perhaps no one would have thought of showing them to me." For the rest of his life Whistler rated Hogarth England's greatest artist.

To escape the heat of St. Petersburg summers, the family moved to a country villa within walking distance of Catherine the Great's magnificent rural palace, Tsarskoé Seló. Mrs. Whistler took her children to see the palace and the pavilions and fountains scattered over the vast, meticulously maintained estate. But the only sight that inspired a comment in her journal was one room in the palace, a Chinese salon designed by Charles Cameron. A Scot who had never visited China, Cameron had nonetheless made of the salon a celestial fantasy in the Oriental style that was then immensely fashionable with European aristocrats. The pastel colors and the painted decorations on the walls —ferns, a bare twig, branches in blossom—were serenely simple. Whistler was later to evoke this same ordered enchantment in his Nocturnes and Arrangements. Whether he was conscious of this early influence is a matter of conjecture, just as it is uncertain whether in his later pictures of fireworks he was recalling that as a child he used to beg to stay up late at night to watch the rockets bursting over the river Neva. We do know that he experienced these delights in Russia, and that they seem to be commemorated in his adult work.

In Russia he also discovered the joys of his own audacity. After an outing to Peter the Great's glittering palace, Peterhof, Mrs. Whistler wrote admiringly of Peter's own painting of birds. But, she added, young Jimmy "was so saucy as to laugh at them." Surely this was the first time that an American youngster had the occasion or the temerity to laugh at the handiwork of Russia's grandest monarch. Yet it certainly was not the last time that Whistler was to hoot his derision. Laughing at the Czar's birds, the boy was tuning up for a lifetime of caustic comment on the works of others.

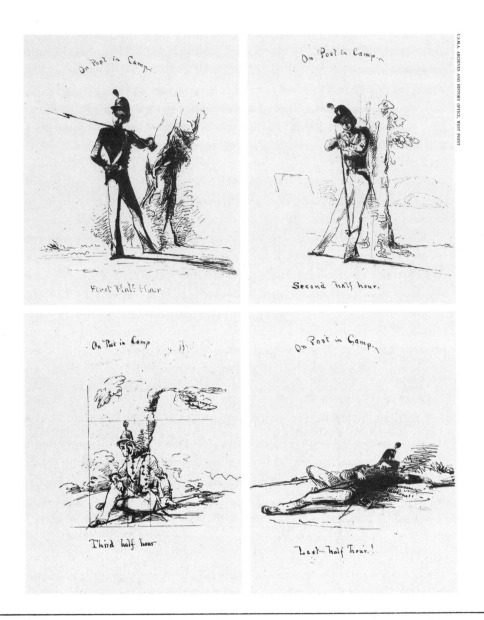

On Post in Camp.

First Half Hour.

On Post in Camp.

Second half hour.

On Post in Camp.

Third half hour

On Post in Camp.

Last half hour!

Although the West Point *Regulations* stated that "cadets should understand the honor and responsibility of a soldier on post," Whistler apparently did not take the rules very seriously. He gave this series of sketches, showing the progress of a bored cadet in two hours on post, to his drawing instructor, who was later killed in the Civil War. The teacher's son found them among his father's effects many years afterward and presented them to the Academy, where they now hang.

On a summer visit to England in 1846 Whistler's half sister, Deborah, met a young Englishman, Dr. Seymour Haden, and married him a year later. The major confessed to his wife that he didn't much like the groom. Nevertheless, this somewhat stuffy but highly successful young surgeon, who enjoyed the arts and was a gifted etcher, was to play an active role in Whistler's life, providing him a haven of comfort and support. While in England for the wedding, the major arranged for one of the Royal Academicians, Sir William Boxall, to do a portrait of his son. It was painted a year later when Jimmy, because of concern over his rheumatic condition—an epidemic of cholera, in addition, had broken out in Russia that winter—was staying in London with the newlyweds. The major never saw the portrait. Just as he finished the Czar's railroad he was stricken by cholera and died soon after of heart failure. When his widow and their son William came to London to pick up Jimmy for the melancholy voyage home to America, their spirits were lifted at least momentarily by a visit to the Academy in Trafalgar Square. There, on exhibit, was Jimmy, looking very pink and proud in his stiff collar, and deceptively angelic.

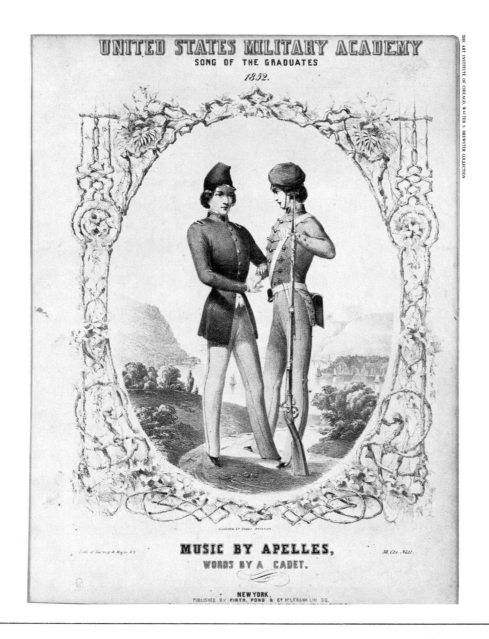

This cover for the sheet music of a school song was the most ambitious drawing Whistler made at West Point. One of the figures was E. P. Alexander, a cadet known as "Little Aleck," who became a Confederate general and later president of a Southern railroad. The other figure was Whistler himself. No one knows which is which, but considering Whistler's insouciance about military procedure, the more commanding figure at left is probably not the future artist but Alexander.

Back in Stonington, Mrs. Whistler faced the fact that the family income had shrunk from $12,000 to $1,500 a year. "The boys were brought up like little princes until their father's death, which changed everything," a relative recalled. Anna Whistler would have preferred to live with her sister, but for the boys' sake she took rooms in a farmhouse in another Connecticut town, Pomfret, near a good school run by a former West Point engineer who had become a parson. In a stalwart effort to direct her sons on the path to salvation, she had them recite Bible verses every morning before breakfast, and exhorted Jimmy to overcome his fits of indolence and help with the farm chores. But Jimmy remained more of a prince than a pauper. At school he ridiculed the principal's high collar by making himself an even higher paper collar that almost hid his ears. This sent the girl students into squeals of mirth and provoked the parson into giving him a caning.

Mrs. Whistler soon decided, probably with relief, that the best place for Jimmy was West Point, where her brother and husband had both flourished. Her stepson, George, petitioned the help of the influential New England lawyer and orator Daniel Webster, the appointment to the Academy was approved by President Millard Fillmore, and 10 days before his 17th birthday, James McNeill Whistler entered West Point, where Colonel Robert E. Lee was then commandant.

The entente between West Point and Cadet Whistler was an unusual one that did them both credit. Whistler was profoundly unmilitary. Yet, as one of the staff generals recalled, "he was a vivacious and likeable little fellow." Another general recalled that he and Whistler had actually painted a picture together. Whistler's own caricatures—of cadets, officers and visitors—were all over the place, and are proudly displayed today in the Academy library. Drawn with a sophisticated economy of line that foreshadows his later inclination to leave out the unimportant, they are mocking in tone, yet simultaneously sympathetic to their subjects. In one, an upperclassman braces a frightened plebe; the upperclassman is the very model of a pompous would-be officer, but an appealing young man nonetheless. And the plebe makes one weep for all the awkward, fat young men who will never quite master the art of the manual of arms. In another sketch, cadets present arms or stand to attention at an encampment; a sly one lounges in the foreground before the duty officer makes his rounds. The drawings are good fun, and they display an affection for the military life that one is surprised to find in facetious young James Whistler. Apparently he, too, thought they were pretty good. When a drawing instructor, brush in hand, tried to correct one of his sketches, he administered a polite rebuke: "Oh don't, sir, don't. You'll spoil it."

Time and again his quips bordered on insubordination. When he was asked at a history quiz the date of the Battle of Buena Vista—an engagement in Mexico in 1847 that redounded to the glory of West Point officers—Whistler pulled a total blank.

"What!" said his instructor. "Suppose you were to go out to dinner, and the company began to talk of the Mexican War, and you, a West Point man, were asked the date of the battle, what would you do?"

"Do?" Whistler shot back. "Why, I should refuse to associate with people who could talk of such things at dinner."

His instructors put up with his guff for three years but were finally forced to call a halt. In his third year Whistler not only flunked chemistry, but accumulated the official total of 218 demerits, a horrendous 18 above the allowable limit—and this after Superintendent Lee (who held the distinction of failing to receive a single demerit while he himself was a cadet) had persuaded several of the officers to remove some of the demerits charged against him. Whistler was dismissed from the Academy. "I can only regret," Lee wrote in a report on the matter, "that one so capable of doing well should so have neglected himself and must now suffer the penalty."

In later years Whistler was fond of telling a somewhat different version of the story. At a chemistry exam, he recalled, he was questioned on the properties of the carbonlike element silicon.

"Silicon is a gas," he replied.

"That will do, Mr. Whistler." And he was dismissed. Ignoring the demerits, he used to say that a correct answer might have changed his life: "Had silicon been a gas, I would have been a major-general."

Yet for the rest of his life Whistler took pride in having attended West Point. It gave him what he needed, a sense of belonging. And it gave him, in the absence of his own father, a group of surrogate fathers who indulged him. He enjoyed wearing the trim cadet uniforms, and he fed on the image of himself as a dashing officer.

It is not surprising, then, that after his dismissal he set out to win his way back into the service. In Washington he called on the Secretary of War, Jefferson Davis, chatted about his father and St. Petersburg, and let it be inferred that his dismissal was really not too serious; it could have happened to any gentleman. The future president of the Confederacy (who had been dismissed from the Point, but later reinstated, for drinking beer) promised to look into the situation and courteously invited Whistler to call again. Covering his bets, Whistler next visited the Secretary of the Navy, proposing without success that he be admitted to Annapolis. Finally, after receiving Lee's report, Davis informed Whistler that it was impossible for him to return to the Point. But the Secretary suggested, in view of the young man's outstanding art record at the Academy—he had been No. 1 in drawing although at the bottom of his class in virtually everything else—that he might fit into the drawing division of the United States Coast Survey. Captain Henry Benham, who was assistant chief of the Survey, turned out to have known Whistler's father, was charmed by this chip off the old major and created a job for him at $1.50 a day.

The benefit to Whistler was great. In the course of making Survey charts, he learned the art of etching and found he had a rare aptitude for the technique, one that he was soon to put to extensive use. But

In 1854, during his brief tour of duty as a cartographer for the U.S. Coast Survey, young Whistler engraved this copper plate. It is an accurate rendering of a part of Boston's harbor, but the bored young cartographer could not resist dressing up a dull chart with the etched doodles at upper left and right. Whistler students find them fascinating; the woman in the oval at left may be an early Whistler's *Mother*. While such whimsical additions annoyed the executives of the Coast Survey, its successor agency, the U.S. Coast and Geodetic Survey, today takes pride in the technical instruction Whistler received while employed in its offices, which he later put to good use when he turned to etching.

aside from keeping the captain amused, Jimmy did him little good. His attendance at the Survey office was sporadic, for his social life kept him very busy. "I was asked and went everywhere," he explained. He could afford only a tiny room on 13th Street and his wardrobe was skimpy. But he made no bones about inviting the Russian Minister to dine, first taking him shopping for the groceries—in the Minister's own carriage, of course—and then gaily cooking the dinner himself in his room. And when he was invited to formal parties for which he had no proper jacket, he pinned back his coattails to achieve approximately the correct, swallow-tailed effect. But it became clear even to him that he was embarrassing Captain Benham; after three months he resigned from the Survey office, bringing himself face to face with the question of his true calling. There could be no doubt; he was an artist. His family agreed. His half brother, George, who now held a good job as an engineer in Baltimore, offered to give him an allowance of $350 a year in quarterly installments, plus passage to France. In the summer of 1855 Whistler set sail.

His choice of destination may have been influenced by reading Henri Murger's *Scènes de la Vie de Bohème*, a collection of tales about the Parisian escapades of young artists; one of these stories provided the plot for Puccini's romantic opera *La Bohème*. At any rate, Whistler arrived in Paris in a jaunty hat and a flowing tie and swept on stage like an operatic hero himself.

He had come to the right city. At this juncture in the development of modern art, Paris was already a place of crucial importance. It was, in current terms, where the action was. Under Emperor Napoleon III the city was growing, thriving, confident. Streets were being widened. New boulevards were cutting across old *quartiers*. The chug and rumble of the Industrial Revolution had begun. Factories, foundries and sooty locomotives threatened to defile beauty and destroy individuality. But these hostile forces gave the artists of Paris a common foe, an adversary powerful enough to be taken on with pride—and with the possibility of a victory worth winning. As a result, Paris inspired a heady camaraderie among its young artists, and encouraged them to work together, love together, carouse together and starve together. Paris was, in short, a city not only of light but of verve and constant change. Any artist could man his own barricade or join a troop of comrades whose principles he admired.

In the summer of Whistler's arrival, Napoleon III was trumpeting his power and progress by the Exposition Universelle, intended partly as an answer to England's celebrated Crystal Palace exposition of 1851. Queen Victoria magnanimously came over for Napoleon III's show and rode around Paris in a carriage with the Emperor and his entrancing Spanish wife, the Empress Eugénie, whose many bedfellows probably gave her less joy than Victoria's one, her prince consort, Albert. For Whistler, however, native or visiting royalty was of less interest than two large exhibits at the Exposition of the paintings of Jean-Auguste-Dominique Ingres and Eugène Delacroix, the grand old men of French art (and archenemies). Along with Gustave Courbet, a firebrand who was displaying 50 of his "realist" works in his own private pavilion outside the Exposition grounds, these painters summed up the shifting currents of French art. Ingres represented the waning Neoclassical strain, Delacroix a free expression of swirling color and personal emotion that was to help bridge the way to modern art. Courbet, for his part, drastically rejected "costume" painting in favor of everyday realism. In due time Whistler wound up a partisan of Courbet, but in later years declared that he wished he had trained under Ingres.

For the moment, Whistler joined the atelier of Charles Gleyre. This academic Swiss painter, a disciple of Ingres, tended to neglect color in favor of meticulous drawing, but still allowed his students some leeway for personal expression—in the best tradition of the Paris atelier system. Under it, the teacher provided his students with a studio apart from his own working quarters, along with a male and female model on alternate weeks. There was no formal instruction, no drawing from the antique like that Whistler had done at the Imperial Academy in St. Petersburg. By drawing directly from life, most students gained a firmer grasp of fundamentals right at the start. The master let them alone except for one or two days a week when he turned up to criticize everybody's work. Frequently, the older students helped the younger ones. As might be expected, these unsupervised ateliers often exploded in wild exhibitions of horseplay, wrestling, calisthenics and sometimes brutal hazing. Whistler claimed in later years that he never took part in such outbursts, and is reputed to have asked some of his English colleagues who were sweating through a session of weight lifting, "Why the devil can't you fellows get your concierge to do that sort of thing for you?"

Whistler soon tired of life in the Gleyre atelier and decided he could learn more profitably in the streets, parks, cafés and dance halls. This led to a charge—one which persisted for a number of years—that he was an idler and dilettante. But his closest associates testified that he was always sketching—peddlers, fruit sellers, beggars, children in the park, girls of the street—always making notes and honing his powers of observation.

Soon Whistler came to epitomize the prankish art student, undaunted in the face of poverty, and he fast became a legend in the Latin Quarter. When he could not afford sketch paper, he visited the bookstalls along the Seine and furtively tore out the blank flyleaves. When he lacked formal footwear to wear to a dinner party, he prowled his hotel hallway, where guests had left their shoes to be shined outside their doors, chose a pair that fitted him and returned the shoes at dawn. When he grew hungry in the last lean days before money arrived from home, he pawned every possible item in his room and triumphantly told a friend, "I have just eaten my washstand." And when funds did arrive, he wined and dined his comrades and gaily bought a hat for a café keeper's pretty daughter.

For two years he lived with Fumette, a much-admired little model who went in for crocheting, reciting poems by Alfred de Musset and losing her temper. After one fiery argument Fumette tore up all his sketches. It was one of the few crises that Whistler did not meet with a joke. He burst into tears.

For male friends, he orbited between the English students, who were more studious, and the French, who were more inspiring. Among the British were several whom he knew for the rest of his life—on terms of diminishing cordiality. They included Edward Poynter, a future president of the Royal Academy; Val Prinsep, a wealthy art patron and painter; and the most interesting of the lot, George du Maurier, who later gained fame as a staff illustrator for the magazine *Punch*. In 1894 du Maurier attained even greater renown as author of the novel *Trilby*, in which the young Whistler was ridiculed as "Joe Sibley," a witty but vain and idle American.

Whistler seemed to be developing faster as a personality than as an artist. But this impression was dispelled when he produced a series of 12 etchings known as *The French Set*, mainly inspired by a tour of northern France, Luxembourg and the Rhineland that he took with a French art-student friend, Ernest Delannoy. Whistler's first efforts reveal a stiffness that reflected his training with the Washington chartmakers, but his exposure to the open road loosened his style and his powers of perception. As a rule, he made no preliminary pencil sketches, but worked directly with his etching needle on wax-covered copper. This meant that instead of carrying a light sketch pad, he was weighed down with heavy plates. But the resulting spontaneity in his work was worth the extra load.

In subject matter the etchings covered what one would expect from an alert young man on a walking tour: a farmhouse kitchen, village streets, landscapes, a tender little portrait, *Gretchen at Heidelberg*, and a moving study, *Peasant Woman*. Even at this early stage of his career, Whistler revealed an ability to catch the inner life of the sitter, and a gift for conveying warmth without sliding into the mawkishness that had been the bane of Romantic art. His touch was light but firm. He neither patronized nor prettified his subjects; rather, he endowed them with dignity and spirit. In these first etchings Whistler displayed his talents more effectively than he did in his early paintings.

On his way to becoming one of the world's finest etchers, Whistler exposed a side that was directly opposite to his outer personality. On the surface he was addicted to overstatement; his flamboyant attire, loud laughter and extroverted exuberance were somehow larger than life. But his best etchings, in their Puritan sparsity of detail, are masterpieces of understatement. It is remarkable how much they express with minimal means, as if the artist had discovered a pictorial shorthand that the beholder reads and mysteriously translates in his own mind. In this regard, Whistler appears intuitively to have discovered a secret of Chinese and Japanese art: the ability to capture essences without palpable devices, or, as a Zen priest once put it, to imply the whole hen by its tracks alone.

Whistler had *The French Set* struck off by a skilled Parisian artisan, Auguste Delâtre, while he stood watching by the old star-wheel press, absorbing every step of the operation. Soon he was able to han-

A memento of student days, this 1894 sketch by George du Maurier contrasts Whistler *(left)* and the Englishman Edward Poynter, both of whom studied art with du Maurier in Paris in the mid-1850s. Looking back 40 years, du Maurier remembered Whistler as a frivolous idler, "vain, witty, . . . eccentric in his attire (though clean), so that people would stare at him . . . which he adored!" Here he strolls the boulevard while the industrious Poynter (who later became a well-known Academician), soberly garbed and loaded with painting gear, trudges to class. The sketch was an illustration for *Trilby*, du Maurier's novel of bohemian life, in which he presented thinly disguised portraits of his artist friends.

"HARPER'S MONTHLY MAGAZINE," 1894, LXXXVIII, P. 579

dle this printing process himself; throughout his life he took pains to master all the technicalities connected with his art. He began selling the *Set* himself, at a price of two guineas (about $10 at the time) for the lot of 12 prints, and apparently succeeded in making a few sales.

Like many clever art students in Paris, Whistler bolstered his small income by copying masterpieces at the Louvre. Captain "Stonington Bill" Williams, an old friend from Connecticut, offered him a flat $25 apiece for as many copies—of anything—as he could turn out. But Whistler picked up more than dollars as a result of these Louvre visits. The museum was crowded with artists, who kept their easels and paints in a special storeroom. Everybody passed through: oldtimers like Delacroix in his lavender gloves, or newcomers like Édouard Manet and Edgar Degas, copying, peering, making friends—as talkative as ancient Greeks in the agora or as college students on the campus.

In 1858 Whistler struck up a conversation at the Louvre with a young painter, Henri Fantin-Latour. The talk flowed on that night at a café, where Fantin-Latour introduced him to another young artist, Alphonse Legros. The three hit it off so well that they formed a group called the "Society of Three," which was to be of continuing benefit to Whistler. His new friends made him aware of the French poet-critic Charles Baudelaire and the celebrated man of letters Théophile Gautier, whose theories on art Whistler would later take as gospel. Baudelaire held that it was not the artist's task simply to depict nature, but to make art out of nature; Gautier believed that art was, and should be, totally independent of, and unrelated to, the public good —thoughts that were to become integral parts of the Whistlerian credo. But this lay in the future. A more immediate benefit came from Courbet, whom Whistler met through the "Society" and who offered instruction to a group of young artists working atelier style in a friend's studio. Whistler joined this group and proclaimed Courbet "a great man." Courbet's effort to find beauty in the ordinary appealed to Whistler, although ultimately they parted company because in Whistler's eyes Courbet's art was too literal, leaving too little to the imagination.

Already Whistler had staked a claim as a realist in his admirable *French Set*, and in two rather clumsy oil portraits of humble people, *La Mère Gérard* and *Head of an Old Man Smoking*. In the proximity of Courbet he blossomed as a painter, and impressed his peers with *At the Piano (pages 30–31)*, a scene painted from memory, showing his half sister, Deborah Haden, and her small daughter, Annie, in their London home. Here was a lovely, poised piece of work. Courbet declared that he approved of it, which meant that in French avant-garde circles Whistler had arrived.

At the Piano was rejected by the Paris Salon of 1859. But with Courbet's encouragement Whistler sent it to London to the Royal Academy, which in 1860 exhibited it in the same gallery where Boxall's portrait of him as a boy had hung. Thus, in the span of 11 years Whistler was twice represented in Great Britain's leading showcase of art. This time he was not merely the subject of a painting, but the author of one, auspiciously launched on what was to be a stormy career.

The French Lessons

The story of Whistler's early years as an artist is a tale of two cities, Paris and London. Leaving his native America for good in 1855 at the age of 21, he plunged happily into the bohemian artistic life of the French capital, sustained by a small stipend from home. Among the friends he made were the painters Henri Fantin-Latour *(right)* and Gustave Courbet, and he also took a French girl as his mistress. Soon a familiar figure in the studios and cafés of the Left Bank, Whistler kept people laughing with his acerbic and witty remarks about art and the world at large, but he never neglected his work. Polishing his skills at drawing, he became a first-class etcher; under the tutelage of Courbet he developed a realistic style of painting. And he also evolved the enchanting tone of isolation and detachment that would always characterize his finest work.

During this period Whistler often visited in London, and he spent more and more time there after Britain's prestigious Royal Academy of Art accepted some of his paintings for exhibition. Eventually he settled in London, continuing his Continental way of life, consorting with avant-garde artists, taking another mistress, an Irish beauty named Jo Heffernan, and winging verbal darts at every handy target. The young American who had arrived in Europe an unknown was embarked upon a career that would in time make every connoisseur aware of the work —and opinions—of James McNeill Whistler.

Arriving one day to visit his friend Fantin-Latour in his underheated garret studio, Whistler found him in bed, with top hat and overcoat on, sketching. Amused at the sight, Whistler dashed off this sketch of the intent painter, noting that Fantin was "pursuing his studies with difficulty—at 14 degrees [C.] cold."

Fantin-Latour in Bed, 1859

27

Fumette, Standing, 1859

Like most impecunious artists, Whistler relied on his friends and relatives to pose for him. Above is an etching of his French mistress, Fumette, posing in a long gown. In the painting at right, his niece, Annie Haden, sits reading; her mother is reflected in the mirror over the mantel and an unidentified woman stands silhouetted in a riding habit. Despite his ties to these people, Whistler portrays them with dispassion; they seem set apart both from one another and from the artist, who treats them simply as elements of composition. This cool vision would emerge as a major quality of Whistler's mature style.

Harmony in Green and Rose: The Music Room, 1860

Edgar Degas: *The Bellelli Family*, c. 1859

Henri Fantin-Latour: *The Two Sisters*, 1859

Among the artists in Whistler's circle in Paris, many were intrigued by a new approach to realism revealed in the works of Courbet and Degas. Both painters were turning from the subjects then popular —classical mythology and romantic adventure—to pursue the character of spontaneous moments in everyday life. Degas presented his version of the new realism in a portrait of his relatives, the Bellellis *(top)*. Defying many of the conventions of family portraiture, Degas has not posed a majestic father surrounded by an adoring brood; rather, he has depicted a scene of domestic tension, in which the mother and one of her daughters seem isolated from the head of the household.

In a somewhat less dramatic manner Whistler's fellow student Fantin-Latour painted the realistic

At the Piano, 1859

portrait *(bottom, left)* of his two sisters, but tinged it with a sadness that was to prove prophetic. Soon after the painting was completed the sister who is shown embroidering, Nathalie, fell seriously ill and spent the rest of her life confined in a sanatorium. The other sister, Marie, who was Fantin's favorite, broke his heart when she left Paris forever to marry a Russian Army officer.

In *At the Piano (above)*, Whistler, too, employed the realistic style, but stamped it with his own special touch of the ethereal. As in *The Music Room (preceding page)*, Whistler's niece and his half sister, Deborah Haden, serve as his models. As the mother plays and the girl listens they seem lost in their private reveries, oblivious of each other; muted hues and filtered light add a haunting glow.

31

The Thames in Ice, 1860

Gustave Courbet: *Stormy Sea*, exhibited 1870

Whistler's friend and mentor Courbet encouraged him to paint directly from nature. He succeeded so well in evocative seascapes like the one below that they provided inspiration for the master himself. Courbet's own later work *(left)* shows his realism softened by the sense of mood caught by the younger man.

Water scenes always fascinated Whistler, and in England he had a love affair with the Thames, celebrating its beauty in frozen winters *(far left)* and balmy summers. In another painting *(overleaf)* he combined a study of the Thames at Wapping with portraits of his mistress Jo, the artist Alphonse Legros and a local sailor. A quiet painting, it captures an isolated moment that is specific yet timeless.

The Blue Wave: Biarritz, 1862

33

Wapping on Thames, 1861–1864

36

II

American on the Thames

All dressed up with no place
to go, this wistful little girl
epitomizes the Victorian taste
for the touching anecdote in
art: raindrops on the window
tell her story. The painter, one
of the few highly successful
women artists in England,
shows great skill in
representing detail with
precision, but the painting
evokes only a minor sentiment.

Sophie Anderson:
No Walk Today, c. 1880

In the spring of 1859 Whistler shifted his base of operations from
Paris to London. It was a fateful decision. Over the years London was
the arena in which he fought his battles for art, a field of combat
where he experienced both deep humiliations and heady victories. London was to be his schoolroom, his stage and even his place of worship,
for his moments of greatest reverence were the quiet evenings he spent
along the Thames, recording the river's bustle and beauty. London,
with all its attractions and exasperations, was where Whistler came of
age as an artist.

Among the major inducements that lured him across the Channel
was the fact that his half sister, Deborah, lived there with her well-to-
do husband, Dr. Seymour Haden. The Haden establishment, a roomy,
four-story, cream-colored brick house at 62 Sloane Street in the
Knightsbridge district, gave Whistler a roof, a bed and sustenance.
There, whenever he wished, he was welcomed into a well-ordered world
where meals were served on time and where he could count on the avun-
cular interest of Haden, 16 years his senior, while basking in the love
of Deborah and their daughter, "wonderful little Annie."

Added to the comforts of Sloane Street were the powerful charms
of the Thames, which enticed Whistler and his brother-in-law into frequent sketching trips along its banks. Once at the river, they would usually go their separate ways. Dr. Haden would walk west to the lush
riverine landscapes that he liked to etch; Whistler turned east to Wapping, the rough London dock area with its webs of rigging, its hubbub
of barges, its salty smells and saltier characters. This part of the lower
Thames was the only territory outside his studios that Whistler ever
claimed as his own. It balanced the civilized and slightly precious
world that he otherwise chose to inhabit. In 1859 he produced several
etchings of the Thames, *his* Thames; they were among the happiest
products of his career *(pages 155, 156-157)*. Sold at the print shop
of one Serjeant Thomas, they greatly enhanced Whistler's reputation.
At this stage he was not yet interested in the river's poetic moods.
Rather, he relished its hectic activity as a port. He took pride in show-

ing the correct rigging of the ships, in depicting craft that looked sea-worthy, in portraying the seafarers and dock workers.

Still another inducement for Whistler to put down stakes in London was the practical fact that the Victorian era was an unusually prof-itable one for artists. For the public, art rendered many services. It made the newly rich, in an age of galloping commercialism, feel that as art buyers they were proving their gentility and culture. In view of the widely held idea, voiced in America by the clergyman Joseph Thompson, that "commerce cannot be entrusted with the moral inter-ests of mankind," art was expected to jump in where commerce failed. It preached sermons, expressed noble sentiments, taught wholesome lessons, and, like Scheherazade dressed up as a Sunday-school teach-er, told moralizing tale after tale. Whistler was totally out of sympathy with the notion of Art as Uplift or Art as Anecdote, but in his op-timism over England's booming art market he overlooked the con-cessions one would have to make to be popular and wrote to Fantin-Latour in Paris, "Come, come, come. Come at once to my house. There you will find everything necessary. . . . England, dear friend, greets young artists with open arms."

By "my house," Whistler meant Haden's house. The doctor, a gen-erous if sometimes overbearing man, seconded the invitation, and opened his arms—perhaps a bit wider than he had anticipated, for Fan-tin-Latour was not the only friend his brother-in-law invited to London. The French bohemian influx into Sloane Street had its comic side. After Fantin-Latour came Ernest Delannoy, Whistler's raggle-taggle hiking companion on the walking tour that produced *The French Set*. Delan-noy was frightened of the Hadens' shower bath, calling it a *"cataracte de Niagara,"* and was convinced that the butler was spying on him. Then there was Alphonse Legros, in so depressed a state over the death of his impecunious father and the debts he had left that Whistler asserted only God could help him.

To these talented vagabonds, all in their twenties, *chez Haden* was a paradise of roast beef, champagne, clean sheets and sympathy. Haden goodheartedly bought some of their paintings, framed the works hand-somely and hung them on his walls. But at one point trouble entered paradise. Haden decided that in one Legros oil he had purchased, a scene of a church interior, the artist had bungled the perspective of the floor. He took the canvas to the studio he had set up for himself on the top floor of his house and made what he thought were needed improve-ments. When Whistler and Legros saw this "impertinence" they sneaked the canvas out of the house and carried it to a studio Whistler had taken in South Kensington. With the help of turpentine, Legros pro-ceeded to restore his own perspective. While he was at work, Haden ar-rived, panting and angry. Whistler defended Legros and Haden had to accept defeat, along with the role, thrust upon him deservedly or not, of an insensitive Philistine.

Haden's lofty assumption of superior knowledge irked Whistler more than once. For a while *At the Piano*—Whistler's study of Deb-orah and her daughter Annie—graced a wall of the Sloane Street house. "But I had no particular satisfaction in that," Whistler recalled some years later. "Haden just then was playing the authority on art, and he could never look at it without pointing out its faults and telling me it would never get to the Academy—that was certain."

Whistler's joy when *At the Piano* was hung at the annual Academy exhibition in 1860 can be imagined. The critic and novelist William Makepeace Thackeray, his daughter reported, "admired it beyond words and stood looking at it with real delight." John Millais, a popular young painter who eventually became the Academy's president, said to Whistler, "I never flatter, but I will say that your picture is the finest piece of color that has been on the walls of the Royal Academy for years." The antagonism between Whistler and Haden grew, and not without justice, it seems, on both sides.

To Whistler's credit he had been aware from the first of the dangers of being constantly underfoot at the Hadens' and had lost no time in finding a studio elsewhere soon after his arrival in London. Later he took a one-room studio-flat in Newman Street, where many artists had rented working quarters, including—about a century earlier—America's Benjamin West. From time to time Whistler sublet his place to his old Paris friend George du Maurier, while he himself took a room in Wapping to soak up more atmosphere for his etchings. Du Maurier reported that his wandering landlord had a habit of popping in on him: "Jimmy made his appearance early on the Sunday morning and sat recounting his experiences for about three hours on my bed. The grandest genius I ever met, a giant." On another occasion the five-foot-four-inch giant spent two nights at the studio and according to du Maurier talked 48 hours without stopping. His "bons mots, which are plentiful," said du Maurier, "are the finest thing I ever heard; and nothing that I have ever read of in Dickens or anywhere can equal his *amazing* power of anecdote."

As in the novels he was later to write, du Maurier had a tendency to romanticize. Whistler was not so much a great coiner of phrases as a master of pace and timing when telling a story. He was a superb mimic, assuming all the parts, taking the hero's role for himself in anecdotes originally told by someone else. He had a favorite one about a hungry Latin Quarter student who had once eaten his landlady's goldfish. In Whistler's version, he was the student, and the landlady had been serving him fish too often. So Whistler baited a hook made from a bent pin, lowered it into the landlady's goldfish bowl, waited patiently for the fish to bite, caught them, fried them and returned them to the bowl with a note to the landlady reading: "Madam, you have cooked so many fish for me that I have ventured to cook some for you." At this point Whistler would add: "She was cured. She gave me no more fish." Then while the company laughed, he would deliver the punch line: "She gave me notice instead." Convulsive laughter, punctuated by the loud "ha-ha's" of the storyteller.

The pleasure Whistler took in his friends, his zest for living, his avidity for turning out pictures, were all inextricably mingled. There were no demarcations between art and life. The same stevedores, sailors

Whistler extended to his artist's tools
the same meticulous care he applied to
his work. He used a dentist's pick as an
etching needle *(top, about two thirds
actual size)* and kept it sharply honed,
protecting the point—and himself—by
punching it into a cork. Whistler's table
palette *(above)* was a model of order;
one friend observed that "the colours
were arranged almost with the
appearance of a picture. In the centre
was white and on one side were the
various reds leading up to black, while
on the other side were the yellows
leading up to blue."

and sea captains he etched on his copper plates might turn up at the
roaring dinners he gave at a Wapping tavern for his fellow artists. At
one party at which the tavernkeeper's wife flirted with Whistler, the artist proposed a toast and made a mock adulatory speech to her husband,
who remained unaware of both the kidding and the flirting. Whistler's
skillful if somewhat underhanded feat of deception reduced his guests
to what one called "fits of laughter." After such a party, he might go
on to the printing establishment of Serjeant Thomas in Bond Street
and work until dawn, sipping a glass of port while he meticulously
pulled his latest Thames etching off the press.

Whistler's life also began to include a beautiful redhead named Jo
Heffernan, and in the paintings he now began to produce she appeared
with increasing frequency. No one knows how they met. Apparently
she was from the Chelsea district of London, daughter of a jovial, whis-
key-loving Irishman who may or may not have been a retired sea
captain, and it is assumed that like many another Chelsea girl she
served as occasional model for the artists of London. At first that was
the relationship between her and Whistler. Then she became his mistress, and her father—jokingly or hopefully—took to referring to
Whistler as "me son-in-law." Jo shared Whistler's bed in his Wapping
room and in his studio flat, and went on sharing it as he went on loving
her and painting her for a decade.

The first important painting in which Jo appears is a scene called
Wapping on Thames (pages 34-35) that he began in 1861. It is a work
that is also interesting because of a paradox it reveals in Whistler,
one that is reflected in later works as well. By nature Whistler was
a gregarious and convivial man; he doted on company even when he
was busy working. Yet in his paintings he was evidently unable to
picture a group of people who seemed to be taking more than the most
desultory interest in one another.

In *Wapping* two men, along with Jo, are seated in a shadowy corner
of a balcony overlooking the Thames. The bearded man is inclining
his head toward the other man, but between them there is no bond of interest, no sign of animation whatsoever. As for Jo, resting against a
railing with her back to the river, she might as well be a thousand miles
away. Whistler once explained the painting by saying that Jo was feign-
ing indifference to pique the younger man. If so, her indifference is so
well feigned that it passes for the real thing.

Solitude despite propinquity is also depicted, and most charming-
ly, in Whistler's 1859 etching *The Music Room*. The scene is a quiet
evening at the Haden home. Deborah sews, Seymour reads a newspaper, and his young medical assistant studies a book. Any one of
them, we feel, could drop dead and the demise would not be noticed
for half an hour. In another Whistler etching, *Soupe à Trois Sous,* five
weary men sitting together in a tiny Paris café are five separate portraits of isolation—and despair.

The length to which Whistler went to avoid face-to-face confron-
tations in his pictures is also demonstrated in a painting called *Harmony in Green and Rose: The Music Room (page 29)*. One of his most

fascinating conceptions, it is again a study of people in their private worlds, a metaphor of individual loneliness. Here little Annie Haden is lost in a book. Beside her, with back turned to the child, is a tall, chic lady in a riding habit. She is being entertained, we infer, by her hostess, Deborah. Only we do not see Deborah. All we catch is her reflection in a large mirror at the left. The two women are not looking at each other at all; they might as well be strangers. Thus, Whistler creates an impression of unrelated images, as if to say that even with three people in a room—and what a normal, cheerful little room it is—no one really communicates with anyone else.

Whether this was his conscious intent, the implications are inescapable. In more direct statements of loneliness, Whistler in the 1860s repeatedly placed a lone figure in an outdoor scene: a girl on a rocky seacoast, a woman in front of a house, a man watching the sea. In part, these pictures of solitary people may be ascribed to Whistler's determination to expel all anecdotal elements from his work, his refusal to tell a story or even to hint the existence of a story. Yet, as other contemporary painters were to prove, it is possible to banish all plot from a picture and still imply a relationship among people. There is no overt evidence that Whistler himself ever suffered from loneliness, except at the death of somebody dear to him. (Once, asked why he looked so glum after the death of a man with whom he had feuded for years, he said: "I'm lonesome. They are all dying. I have hardly a warm personal enemy left.") Yet his pictures are an unconscious expression, one surmises, of a hidden isolation—of an inability, for all his social gifts, to engage in a genuine interchange of emotion. He remained the showman at center stage, never without an audience, but perhaps as lacking in true companions as are the people in his paintings.

Probably the most effective companion in Whistler's life, at least for a while, was Jo Heffernan. She was not only mistress but all-purpose household angel—cooking, keeping accounts, fending off tradesmen who demanded to be paid, helping to scrimp when Whistler was poor and splurge when he was rich, going everywhere with him except to nice Victorian homes like the Hadens'.

Jo had self-respect and dignity, and some other admirable qualities as well. She liked to improve herself, to read, to draw. She often accompanied Whistler on his Thameside expeditions and sold some of her own sketches of the waterfront under the name of Mrs. Abbott, the baptismal name that Whistler had dropped. She did not react overdramatically to his occasional spells of promiscuity. In the early 1860s Whistler sired, by an unknown woman, a son who was named John, and to whom he frankly referred as "my infidelity to Jo." Jo generously adopted John and raised him. He called her "Aunty," and eventually he became a successful engineer. At about the same time, Jo bore her own child by Whistler, a boy named Harry. Dates and details about Harry are sparse and what happened to him is not known.

Perhaps Jo's most satisfying duty was posing for Whistler; her Irish beauty is enshrined in several of his most celebrated works. Whistler was often tyrannical with his models, heedless of their aching muscles

Although she posed for Whistler many times, Jo Heffernan was rarely pictured with as much affection as in *Weary*, an 1863 etching. The woman who for about 10 years lived and traveled with Whistler, while excluded from some social circles, exerted a strong influence on him. For example, though she had posed with Alphonse Legros for the painting *Wapping on Thames (pages 34-35)*, it was Jo's dislike of Legros that probably prompted Whistler to end his long friendship with the other artist.

and bodily needs. Jo beat the game one day by falling asleep during a sitting, but Whistler beat the game too by seizing the opportunity to produce a wonderful little etching called *Weary*. As Jo nestles back in a comfortable chair, her full skirt billows out in an almost formless froth. But form is amply explicit in the roundness of her breasts under a tight bodice and in her carefully waved hair that radiates like a nimbus and rests neatly on the high back of the chair. Did Whistler steal up and arrange it while she slept? Surely, yes.

Whistler's hopes that he would profit in England's bullish art market were fulfilled, although modestly. He sold *At the Piano* for £30 to a man who had admired it at the Academy exhibition, and he disposed not only of prints of *The French Set* but of some of his Thames etchings. In addition, he managed to acquire some generous friends, including Alexander Ionides, an affluent Greek businessman whose son, Luke, Whistler had met in Paris. The Ionideses entertained him frequently and introduced him to potential buyers. Also among his first patrons was Serjeant Thomas, who began collecting his works.

By the summer of 1861 Whistler was able to finance 15 months of travel in France with Jo. They stopped first in Brittany, where he painted the first of his major paintings of the sea, a recurring subject in his art. *The Coast of Brittany* reflected the realistic trend in French art most forcefully represented by Courbet. With its clutter of rocks and its careful painting of the distant surf this is the most detailed outdoor picture Whistler was ever to produce; he soon tended more and more toward simplicity and abstraction. But there is no denying that this transitional work, with its hint of Victorian sentimentality in the peasant girl sleeping alone on the empty beach, has considerable appeal. It was exhibited the next year at the Academy show in London.

From Brittany, Whistler and Jo went on to Paris. Purposely, it would seem, he avoided the Left Bank haunts of his student years and took quarters in the more conservative Boulevard des Batignolles. He introduced Jo to Courbet and made her unloose her glorious red hair for the Frenchman's inspection. That Courbet approved is obvious from his portrait of Jo, *La Belle Irlandaise (The Beautiful Irish Girl)*, which shows her musing in a mirror and fingering her tresses.

In later years, as Whistler moved away from realism, he denied that he had been influenced by Courbet and in general deplored the older man's approach to art. Nonetheless, Courbet in 1865 wrote a letter to his father in which he referred to Whistler as "my pupil." Courbet did not claim that Whistler had enrolled under him—he never took formal students—but still he felt that his influence on Whistler was strong enough to warrant calling him a pupil. The best evidence on the matter lies in Whistler's early paintings, especially his portraits of the old flower seller, *La Mère Gérard*, and the weather-beaten *Head of an Old Man Smoking*. In Whistler's choice of earthy subjects and bold brushwork, the two works indeed testify to Courbet's influence.

Whistler's major work at this juncture, however, was predominantly his own creation. It was another portrait of Jo, a study in white that he eventually named *Symphony in White No. 1 (page 60)*. In spirit the painting is close to the mood of a poem about a girl by Théophile Gautier, entitled "Symphony in White Major." There is little doubt that Whistler knew this poem, since Gautier was a lion in Paris art circles at the time. But while Gautier's girl was "a Madonna of the snows," Whistler's Jo was no shivering madonna but a smoldering coal.

To provide the background for her that he wanted, he hung a white cloth at the end of his studio and spread a white fur rug over the flowered carpet. In a letter to a friend, du Maurier described Whistler at work: "He is painting the woman in white, red-haired party, life-size . . . beautiful white cambric dress standing against a window which filters the light through a transparent white muslin curtain . . . barring the red hair . . . one gorgeous mass of brilliant white." In a later note du Maurier reported: "The woman in white is nearly finished—Jim working at it all the winter [1861-1862] from eight in the morning got painters' colic very severely."

To repair the ravages of painters' colic—a violent intestinal upset caused by lead poisoning, perhaps brought on in this case by exposure to heavily leaded white paint—Whistler and Jo left for the south of France, planning to go on to Madrid to see the paintings of Velázquez. On the way, to help restore Whistler's health, they stopped off on the Atlantic coast near Biarritz, where he painted a striking work known as *The Blue Wave: Biarritz (page 33)*. In contrast to his first seascape, this new painting was far less detailed, far more his own interpretation of nature than a straightforward imitation of it. Solid rocks, pounding surf and a boiling thunderhead are orchestrally combined to create a quick, single impression of tremendous power.

Painting directly from nature, Whistler felt, demanded a more spontaneous technique than that used indoors in the studio. Like the Impressionists who were then causing a stir in France, he believed that he must learn to use paint sketchily, to make his interpretation on the wing, as it were. To his regular confidant, Fantin-Latour, he wrote: "These pictures painted out of doors after nature, *en plein air,* cannot be anything else than large sketches; a bit of floating drapery, a wave, a cloud, it's there for a moment, then it disappears and the true tone has to be caught in flight just as one shoots a flying bird. But the public demands finished works."

These were significant words, portending more for Whistler's art than he realized. He thought he was asserting only the artist's right to paint nature more in accordance with his own feelings about it, rather than simply duplicating its appearance on canvas. But he was also anticipating the modern artist's total freedom—even from nature. In accord with his expressed hope, Whistler did learn to use paint "as one shoots a flying bird," catching a mood as it raced by. And in the future, just as he foresaw, the public would accuse him over and over of not "finishing" his work.

Unaccountably, Whistler and Jo never got to Madrid. For one thing, Fantin-Latour, who planned to join them in Spain, found at the last minute that he could not leave Paris. For another, Whistler may have taken a dislike to traveling; he had a scare when he almost drowned in

George du Maurier drew this elaborate program for a playlet Whistler and his friends put on as an evening's amusement. Whistler had a knack for finding patrons who would not only buy his works but also invite him into their social circles; *The Thumping Legacy,* for example, was only one of several plays that followed regular Sunday dinners at Tulse Hill, the London home of the wealthy Greek merchant and art collector Alexander Ionides.

a pounding sea until Jo, aided by a burly bystander, pulled him out by the foot. Whatever cut short the journey, the couple returned to Paris and Whistler resumed working on *Symphony in White*.

He submitted it, along with two other paintings and an etching, to the Academy exhibition in London in 1862. The two more orthodox paintings, *The Coast of Brittany* and *The Thames in Ice (page 32)*, were accepted, as was a Thames etching, *Rotherhithe*—no small accomplishment for a relatively unknown young artist who was not a member of the Academy. But *Symphony in White* was snubbed.

Over the years many of Whistler's paintings were to receive only limited recognition, but unlike Thomas Gray's churchyard flower, they were not born to blush unseen. A few months after the Academy jury's rejection of *Symphony in White*, it was prominently hung at the opening of the new Berners Street Gallery in London. The Gallery had been founded, as the London *Athenaeum Journal* put it, "with the avowed purpose of placing before the public the works of young artists, who may not have access to the ordinary galleries." As if to emphasize this point the catalogue of the opening show noted that Whistler's painting had been refused by the Royal Academy. However, among the other artists whose works were on display were such conventional favorites as William Frith, Edward Poynter and Augustus Egg, and so the new gallery was not exactly a hotbed of youthful daring. Rather, its exhibition largely represented the art world that Whistler had to confront, combat and—he hoped—conquer.

The immensely popular Frith was a master of crowded canvases, such as *The Derby Day (pages 50-51)*, as full of people and vignettes as a Dickens novel. Frith specialized in modern themes done in a realistic style and was marvelously accurate in his details of costumes. He composed his crowd scenes with the skill of a fine movie director, and although he had neither the bite nor intensity of England's greatest genre painter, William Hogarth, he caught so winningly the flavor of Victorian England that only a fool would have refused to take some pleasure in his pictures. Whistler admired Frith's work until it became apparent that the anecdotal realism he espoused was inimical to the Whistlerian credo of serving up beauty for its own sake.

The paintings of Augustus Egg were less cluttered than Frith's, but they also were wedded to the storytelling concept. In *Past and Present (page 52)*, Egg offered not just one but three pictures recording the downfall of an unfaithful wife. The scenes show, in sequence, the confrontation between the wronged husband and the wife at the moment he learns of her infidelity, their saddened daughters musing after the father's death (presumably of shock), and, finally, the treacherous, now-homeless widow grieving over the folly of her act and her separation from their children. Yes, it was storytelling time in English art.

It was natural, then, that viewers of Whistler's *Symphony in White* should wonder what tale it intended to tell. Why did the subject project such a mingled impression of purity and violence, with her fiery hair like a bloodstain against the white curtain? Was she, perhaps, haunted by a dead lover? An obliging critic provided the answer by

Insouciantly dangling a leg, Whistler completes a letter *Q* that George du Maurier drew as a decorative initial for *Punch*. Du Maurier, a member of the Chelsea coterie, was for 36 years a staff illustrator on the humor magazine, progressing from small drawings to gentle lampoons of London society.

saying that Whistler was attempting to pictorialize the theme of Wilkie Collins' popular suspense-filled new novel, *The Woman in White*.

Whistler replied to the critique in a letter to the press, the first of hundreds he would dispatch over the years. In this first riposte he began mildly enough: "I had no intention whatever of illustrating Mr. Wilkie Collins' novel; it so happens indeed that I have never read it." Then he took on a tone of mockery, as if spelling out a simple truth to a moron: "My painting simply represents a girl dressed in white, standing in front of a white curtain." Period.

For the English public, convinced as it was that art should be either anecdotal or uplifting or both, Whistler's letter was a slap in the face, and the kind of slap he would deliver again and again. On one occasion he entered an exhibit of popular paintings full of homey scenes and spoke out as if reciting slowly from a primer: "See, the little girl has a pussy cat . . . and that little girl has a broken toy; there are real tears rolling down her cheeks."

Foreseeably, Whistler became gradually less welcome in genteel art circles. He went on venting his scorn with an impish grin, dropping his monocle—an affectation adopted in his Paris student days —with a wicked glitter as he mockingly raised his eyebrow at the work of his opponents. People began to edge away from him.

After *Symphony in White's* debut at the Berners Street Gallery, Whistler rolled up his canvas and carried it to Paris, where in Fantin-Latour's studio he had it reframed for the 1863 Salon. He had cause to expect that at the French exhibition his masterpiece might be viewed a bit more appreciatively. For, unlike the English, the French were slowly becoming less obsessed with subject matter. They had been exposed to the doctrine of Art for Art's Sake.

This troubling concept was really not new. The idea that beauty was independent of usefulness or the public good had been expounded by the greatest of ancient Greek philosophers, Plato and his pupil, Aristotle. More recently, in France, the same basic idea had been advanced with fresh bravura by Théophile Gautier in 1835, in the preface to his novel *Mademoiselle de Maupin*. In the mood of defiance and disenchantment that followed the Napoleonic Wars, Gautier at 24 had lashed out at the dull new utilitarian values of the bourgeois. "There is nothing really beautiful," he asserted, "save what is of no possible use. Everything useful is ugly, for it expresses a need, and man's needs are low and disgusting, like his own poor wretched nature. The most useful place in the house is the water-closet."

Gautier asserted that it was neither the function nor the responsibility of art to help or cure anything. His attitude, it should be noted, was not shared merely by a few avant-garde Frenchmen. It was reflected in America in 1839 in the words of Ralph Waldo Emerson, "Beauty is its own excuse for being," and in the same period by Edgar Allan Poe, who asserted his firm conviction that in art the major heresy was *"the teaching of a lesson."*

But even though Gautier's idea had its supporters abroad, and a special champion in Paris in the brilliant young man of letters Charles

Baudelaire, the doctrine of Art for Art's Sake was not widely accepted either in the New World or the Old. For one thing, accepted criteria of art appreciation were hard to vanquish: ever since art began it had been telling stories and serving "useful" purposes—religious or secular. For another thing, enjoying art abstractly, without benefit of sentiment or association, demanded more effort than most people, including art critics, could muster.

Whistler's *Symphony in White* was turned down by the Salon of 1863, just as it had been by the Royal Academy. Then it took the spotlight in a remarkable event in art history. The entries of a number of young French painters, including Manet, Legros and Fantin-Latour, were also rejected by the Salon, and cries of protest arose from the Parisian intelligentsia. Napoleon III, anxious to demonstrate his liberalism, responded by offering exhibition space in the same building where the official Salon was to be held and at the same time. This new showcase would be called the Salon des Refusés—for the pictures refused by the official Salon. Whistler, who was then on a brief jaunt to Amsterdam with Legros, was enthralled with the idea; it was the kind of theatrical situation he relished. He was fearful only that his Paris dealer, to whom he had entrusted *Symphony in White* for submission to the official Salon, might decide to exhibit the painting in a private gallery after its refusal and thus keep it from what would now be the main circus.

Symphony was, however, shown at the Salon des Refusés and proved an enormous success, the crowd catcher of the exhibit along with Manet's *Déjeuner sur l'herbe (Luncheon on the Grass)*, which became a milestone in modern art. According to some reports, Whistler's work attracted even more outrage than Manet's. Many viewers laughed at *Symphony*. As Émile Zola described the exhibit in his realistic novel *L'Oeuvre: "The Woman in White* [as *Symphony* was first known] . . . was rarely without her group of grinning admirers digging each other in the ribs and going off into fits of helpless mirth."

That Manet's work raised an uproar was understandable; the sight of a naked woman picnicking with two fully, formally clothed gentlemen shocked even Paris. But the agitation over Whistler's painting is less easy to explain, unless it was that the picture's very lack of a plot suggested that it had a hidden story too scandalous to tell. And, as throughout art history, its very originality stirred hostility.

No longer could Whistler complain only about the British; it seemed that the French, too, were hell-bent to read nonsense into his art. They insisted on seeing the girl in white as a vision, a ghost or a medium. One perspicacious critic, Jules-Antoine Castagnary, suspected the horrid truth: that Whistler was concerned solely with harmony of color and form. Castagnary cried out: "Let me see in your work something loftier, *The Bride's Tomorrow,* that troubling moment when the young woman questions herself, and is astonished at no longer recognizing in herself the virginity of the night before."

However absurd these reactions now seem, at least they helped make Whistler one of the two most talked-of painters in Paris in 1863—a circumstance that of course delighted him. As for the Salon des Refusés, that was its first and last showing; Napoleon III had noted the public's disapproval. Even the Empress Eugénie, who was scarcely a prude in her private life, found *Luncheon on the Grass* immodest.

Labels were as much a bore and a bane to Whistler as classifications, but when the French critic Paul Mantz, who rated *The Woman in White* the most important picture of the Refusés, referred to it as a *"symphonie du blanc,"* the phrase stuck in Whistler's mind. He officially changed the title to *Symphony in White No. 1.* Later he painted three more Symphonies in White, and it was, in part, Mantz's happy phrase that led him to seize on other musical terms, and call other works Nocturnes, Caprices, Harmonies and Arrangements. These were more than just handy titles, however. They awakened the public to the abstract elements in Whistler's work and suggested that his paintings might be enjoyed on the same abstract basis as a piece of music. The musical titles not only served Whistler's purposes well, but also helped pave the way for a clearer understanding and greater popular acceptance of the far more abstract art that was to come.

But *Symphony in White* was as yet only a hint of the direction Whistler was to take. In it he veered away from his French-inspired realism toward a more decorative, personal style, with a boldness and dramatic authority quite his own.

If Whistler drew catcalls from the public when *Symphony* was first seen in 1863, he fared better that same year from his peers. In sign of his growing acceptance in the artistic community, he was asked to join a group portrait Fantin-Latour had decided to paint in homage to Delacroix, who had died in August of 1863. Fantin-Latour had been so incensed by the meager attendance at the funeral that he resolved to pay a tribute of his own to the late master by way of a study of 10 rising young men of arts and letters gathered around a portrait of Delacroix. It may seem odd that Delacroix, committed as he was to storytelling art, should attract homage from young rebels who had little respect for it. Yet it was also he, above all, who had preached the gospel of individual expression, "the impulses of the heart," and who had defended both Courbet and Manet against his fellow Academicians.

On Fantin-Latour's canvas, Whistler turned out to be the scene-stealer, holding stage center in one of the best portraits ever made of him. At 29 he is very much the dandy in his frock coat, his hand resting elegantly on the gloves folded over the head of his cane. His slight smile, caught here before its mischief soured to malice, is boyishly engaging. It almost seems that this picture, which was shown at the 1864 Paris Salon, should by rights be called *Hommage à Whistler.*

That Whistler was the only non-Frenchman in a galaxy including Manet, Baudelaire, Legros and Fantin-Latour himself was due in part, of course, to his friendship with Fantin-Latour. But there is no question that he was also in the picture on his own merits. With his usual aplomb he felt perfectly at home among the rising stars of French art. Yet at the same time he was being drawn tighter to England, where a quite different situation in art prevailed.

Victoria's Painters

While young painters like Whistler were struggling to establish themselves in 19th Century London, many more popular artists enjoyed a booming market. Painting to suit the pleasure (as Henry James put it) "of the British merchant and paterfamilias and his excellently regulated family," they won fortunes, honors and even titles. With a high degree of skill they produced works of meticulous naturalism catering to a broad popular taste for a variety of subjects: scenes from contemporary life, anecdotes of home and hearth, moral preachments, parables of virtue and vice, and narrative-packed literary compositions. Biblical, historical and mythological themes rounded out their repertoires—and offered opportunities to paint the female nude, whose eroticism they veiled, sometimes quite thinly, in archeological detail and classical paraphernalia.

That British art of this period was essentially naïve and virtuous is not surprising. The chief arbiters of Britain's taste were her naïve and virtuous sovereigns, Queen Victoria and the handsome Prince Albert. Like their subjects, Victoria and Albert enjoyed paintings that reproduced the everyday world with fidelity, if sometimes through rosy glasses; and they appreciated sentiment far more than passion. Above all, they wanted art to educate and uplift its viewers. Filling this bill of particulars was not easy, but for the artist who could manage it, the rewards of fame and fortune waited.

A microcosm of the Victorian world, this detail from *The Derby Day* shows part of the variegated crowd that gathered on Epsom Downs to watch England's most celebrated horse race, the annual contest founded in 1780 by the 12th Earl of Derby. The wealth of anecdote and detail in the full painting *(overleaf)* made it a gallerygoer's delight for years.

William Powell Frith: *The Derby Day*, detail

Packed with action and color, William Frith's seven-foot-four-inch panorama of a day at the races focuses on the people rather than the sport. Just to the right of center is the main anecdote: the acrobat, who has come with his son to earn a few shillings, finds the boy so distracted by the rich picnic fare being laid out nearby that he cannot perform. At the left, a beseeching wife tries to drag her curious husband away from the tempting shell game that has already, one suspects, emptied the pockets of the top-hatted lad standing dejectedly by. Throughout the scene, dandified gents—their club colors tied jauntily around their hats—flirt with ladies and place bets.

Frith spent nearly two years on the painting. After working out the general composition, he hired a photographer to record at the track "as many queer

groups of people as he could." Adding these pictures to his own recollections, Frith painted the major figures in his studio using live models. The final composition was fitted together like a mosaic.

When *The Derby Day* was exhibited at the Royal Academy in 1858 it proved so fascinating that for the first time in 36 years a railing had to be erected to keep a jostling public from damaging the canvas.

For Frith, the success was stimulating but not entirely new; four years earlier his first essay in painting such wide-scale, highly detailed views of life was bought by Queen Victoria herself. Elected to the Royal Academy in 1853 to fill the seat left vacant by the death of Turner, Frith many years later summed up his own career: he had never been a great artist, but "I am a very successful one."

William Powell Frith: *The Derby Day*, 1856–1858

51

Augustus Leopold Egg: *Past and Present I, II and III*, 1858

Sermons in paint intrigued the Victorian picture-buying public almost as much as realistic tours de force. The popular Augustus Egg adopted a serial approach: his melodrama of marital infidelity *(left, above)* is presented in three acts. Scene 1 represents the past: a stunned husband reads a letter detailing his wife's unfaithfulness; she lies sobbing at his feet

as the children look up from building a house of cards, a symbol of the flimsiness of this broken marriage. Scenes 2 and 3 offer a simultaneous view of the present: years have passed and the daughters mourn their father's death *(center)* while the derelict wife and her illegitimate child shiver *(below)* beneath a dockside archway; the waxing moon hints

Robert Braithwaite Martineau: *The Last Day in the Old Home*, 1862

of future hope. So sad was Egg's story that he was never able to sell it; it was simply "too painful to please," one contemporary explained.

By contrast with Egg's three-part sermon, Robert Martineau's most famous work crowds enough material for a four-volume novel into one canvas. His preachment is against drink and gambling. A family's estate—its worthless deed lying on the floor to the right—is being sold to pay the heir's debts. While his mother relinquishes her keys, the family treasures—already tagged for the auctioneer—are carried away. Meanwhile, the wastrel, at right, toasts a hazardous future and begins debauching his young son with a glass of champagne.

53

Philip Hermogenes Calderon: *Broken Vows*, 1856

James (Jacques) Joseph Tissot: *The Last Evening*, 1873

Heart-warming and heartbreaking romance were eminently popular themes in late-19th Century pictures. In Philip Calderon's baleful scene at left, a stunning young brunette swoons against a garden wall, clutching her side, as her fiancé dallies with a pretty blond thing behind the gate where once he carved their initials. On the ground is the bracelet she had dropped, causing her to stop and overhear the treachery. The picture, rendered in precise detail, was Calderon's first great success: he was only 24 when it was exhibited.

Even more exquisitely detailed, and equally filled with romantic incident, is James Tissot's elegant painting above. A Frenchman who came to England in 1871 as a refugee from his country's political troubles, Tissot exploited a highly polished realistic technique in scenes of social drama. Here, against a backdrop of faultlessly drawn rigging and masts, a young girl listens as two old codgers gossip intently about the couple mooning in the foreground at the end of a shipboard romance. Are they whispering about some event during the cruise, an unseemly public display of affection? Such questions lend the picture considerable anecdotal interest. In fact the young lover is Tissot himself and the lady his beloved Mrs. Kathleen Newton, whose death from tuberculosis at 28, a few years after he painted the scene, devastated the artist.

Frederick, Lord Leighton: *Flaming June*, exhibited 1895

Scenes from classical antiquity provided the painters of the Victorian era with a varied subject matter of considerable current interest plus an excuse to paint beautiful women in stages of undress. Frederick Leighton and Lawrence Alma-Tadema were among many distinguished academic painters who concentrated in this area, earning large fortunes and splendid honors in the bargain: Leighton was England's first artist elevated to the peerage; Alma-Tadema, a naturalized Netherlander, was knighted for his contribution to the arts. Artistically, however, the men were quite different.

In the painting above, for example, Leighton employs a classical setting and costume not to tell a story but to convey an effect. Here, the grace of the slumbering figure and the warm glowing color speak of summer's languor; the woman is voluptuous without being lascivious. Sometimes accused of lacking passion as an artist, Leighton in this picture has clearly adopted the true classical spirit of ennoblement through the calm perception of beauty.

Alma-Tadema was somewhat more down to earth in his aspirations. Fascinated by archeological sites he had seen in Italy, he set out to re-create scenes from everyday life in the ancient world. And he did so with fidelity; his house was filled with artifacts and photographs and each picture was the product of careful research. The charming seminude scene at the right, one of a series of paintings he did on the Roman baths, depicts an *apodyterium*, Latin for the undressing room at the entrance to the bath itself.

Sir Lawrence Alma-Tadema: *An Apodyterium*, exhibited 1886

Peopled with a cast of thousands, presented in glorious color, Sir Edward Poynter's 10-foot panorama showing the oppressed Israelites toiling under the whips of Egypt held enormous appeal for a pre-cinematic Bible-reading public. Everyone was familiar with the passages from Exodus describing Israel's Egyptian bondage: "And they built for Pharaoh treasure cities." Poynter achieved his first substantial success with ambitious scenes from the

times of the pharaohs, and this spectacular painting is the grandest of them all.

Like Leighton and Alma-Tadema, Poynter was an indefatigable researcher, careful to make each detail of his work as authentic as possible—from the hieroglyphics on the obelisk to the creaking, archaic cross-bound wheels of the monument-bearing wagon. But he had erred without knowing it. The painting was bought by a civil engineer, Sir John Hawkshaw,

58

Sir Edward John Poynter: *Israel in Egypt*, 1867

who calculated that Poynter's Israelite work gang was too small to haul the colossal red-sandstone lion sculpture. Accordingly, Poynter corrected the error by adding more slaves up to the edge of the canvas, and implying still more out of sight to the right. Hawkshaw was evidently satisfied by the added manpower.

Poynter also made a concession to the current taste for moral enrichment in paintings by including,

in the central foreground, a compassionate scene of an exhausted slave being offered water while a whip-bearing overseer stands by.

With his many skills, his adaptability and his keen awareness of his audience, Poynter achieved great success; not a single unsold canvas remained in his studio at his death in 1919. Knight, baronet, Royal Academy president for 22 years, he was the last exponent of a dying era's taste.

III

Brotherhood of Radicals

When Whistler returned to his London base in 1864 after paying his homage to Delacroix in Paris, he found himself more and more swept up in the charms of life in the city's bohemian Chelsea district. His chief guide to this artistic circus was Dante Gabriel Rossetti, the painter-poet. Rossetti lived down the street from the house Whistler rented at No. 7 Lindsey Row, and they saw each other often. The two men had much in common. Each had a lordly air, yet a touch of the rogue and mountebank. Each loved nonsense and lively dinner parties. Each had an eye for pretty women, particularly redheads. In specific matters of art, Whistler and Rossetti did not always agree, but they shared an irrepressible urge to question artistic dogma.

Rossetti had been the driving force in one of the most remarkable movements in the annals of art, the Pre-Raphaelite Brotherhood, a small band of young bloods organized to do battle with what they regarded as the sham standards of contemporary British painting. The Brotherhood had been founded before Whistler left America and had lasted barely six years. But its afterglow lived on in an atmosphere of individualism and intense dedication to the arts that Whistler found highly congenial. Unorthodox, outspoken, iconoclastic, the Brothers had injected a fresh breeze into the English art world.

Essentially, what had brought the Brotherhood into being was the tepidness of English painting of the time. The great age of Turner and Constable had waned. At the Royal Academy, Britain's citadel of art, originality was in short supply. The tendency among Academicians was to play it safe. Such men as Daniel Maclise and William Powell Frith were able painters, and justifiably popular as expert practitioners of what had become the favored Victorian style—anecdotal and formularized. They and their colleagues largely concentrated on producing *"tableaux vivants"*—groups of figures theatrically deployed as in a stage-set, painted in murky colors and illuminated with little regard for natural light. Rules of form and perspective, as passed down by Raphael and other great Renaissance masters, were scrupulously followed. Typical Academy paintings were slick, skill-

BIRMINGHAM MUSEUM AND ART GALLERY, ENGLAND

I have been here before,
  But when or how I cannot tell:
I know the grass beyond the door,
  The sweet, keen smell,
The sighing sound, the lights around
  the shore.

You have been mine before—
  How long ago I may not know:
But just when at that swallow's soar
  Your neck turned so,
Some veil did fall—I knew it all of yore.

Has this been thus before?
  And shall not thus time's eddying
    flight
Still with our lives our loves restore
  In death's despite,
And day and night yield one delight
  once more?

ful and—in the eyes of their few detractors—depressingly stale.

Unknown to the Academicians, dissent was brewing under their very noses. Among the fledgling painters at the Academy school in the 1840s there were three who were particularly ripe for rebellion: the flamboyant Rossetti, son of an Italian political refugee; William Holman Hunt, earnest, plodding, acutely aware of the pinch of English lower-class poverty; and handsome John Everett Millais, son of a well-to-do merchant, a boy wonder who, at 11, had been the youngest student ever admitted to the Academy school.

For all their differences in personality and background, Rossetti, Hunt and Millais shared some traits common to the young of all eras. They were romantic, high-minded, inclined to moralize, certain their elders had made a mess of things, especially by allowing the Industrial Revolution to disfigure and complicate English life; they longed for a return to simple virtues—those, for example, of medieval times. The restive youth of late-20th Century America, chafing at their own computerized age, might scent kinship in these ideas; Rossetti, in fact, was a kind of prototype of today's hippie. One of his classmates later wrote that his "thick, beautiful and closely curled masses of rich, brown, much-neglected hair fell . . . almost to the wearer's shoulders," and that his boots were "not over-familiar with brushes."

The same stern judgments that the young rebels leveled against England's industrialism applied also to its art. They did not disdain the great Raphael, idol of the Academicians, but they did scorn those who slavishly followed what they felt was his preference for beauty over truth. Art, they believed, needed to be revitalized, reinvested with meaning, made to serve the cause of "justice and truth." By truth they meant truth to nature, meticulously recorded by painters who were prepared to "look at the world without eyelids," unblinking.

Of the trio of revolutionaries it was Hunt who fixed on the means by which these beliefs could be translated into action. He resolved to paint nature with loving, microscopic accuracy and in bright, "pure" colors rather than in the subdued, "old master" hues that the Academy deemed correct. This was, in effect, the essence of what became Pre-Raphaelitism—an insistence that a faithfulness to nature—to her colors, to her light, to the situations she presented to the eye of the observer —should be the painter's pre-eminent concern. In a sense, this view of art was not unlike that held by the proponents of the artistic revolution gathering strength across the Channel in France. But while the French painters preached the same doctrine of "truth to nature," they were far more interested in conveying general mood and effect than in rendering specific detail.

One evening at Millais' studio, where Rossetti and Hunt often visited, they noticed a book of engravings Millais had acquired, reproducing the religious frescoes that a number of largely anonymous medieval Italian artists had painted at the Campo Santo, the cemetery at Pisa. The engraved copies were poor, but the style of painting they revealed was an eye opener. The Pisan frescoes were simple, forthright, uninhibited by the rules that were later to become Renaissance canon. Perspective was distorted and anachronism abounded; Moses and Adam might appear in the same painting. Moreover, the medieval artists gave the same painstaking attention to secondary as to principal characters. The result was a singular reality, a freshness in striking contrast to the paintings held up to Academy students as the models they should strive to emulate.

A month after this stunning discovery the Pre-Raphaelite Brotherhood was formally established. Rossetti had talked his two cohorts into tapping four more members, probably because he craved to surround himself with a more sizable cabal. The new recruits were Rossetti's brother, William, who in time was to turn to art criticism; a sculptor, Thomas Woolner; and two painters, James Collinson and Frederick George Stephens, who at 19 had never finished a painting but who showed, according to Hunt, "future zeal."

Of the seven Brothers, the oldest was 23. Along with their undoubted talent and seriousness of purpose, they had the coltishness of college students. At the meeting at which they officially dubbed themselves the "Pre-Raphaelite Brotherhood," they took an oath never to reveal the meaning of P.R.B. They agreed, moreover, to put the sacred initials on all their works. Rossetti and Hunt hoped to find a special clubhouse, on the front door of which they planned to paint the letters P.R.B. If callers asked what these meant, the proper reply was to be "Please Ring Bell."

The Brotherhood decided to make its public debut at the annual Academy exhibition of 1849. Fully expecting to be bruised and battered by the critics, only the three original founders proposed to submit entries. Millais' was *Lorenzo and Isabella*, illustrating a poem by Keats; Hunt's was *Rienzi*, inspired by a popular novel by Frederick Bulwer-Lytton; and Rossetti's *The Girlhood of Mary Virgin (page 70)*. All three works were painted in the bright colors frowned on by the Academy, and all three were scrupulously detailed. *Lorenzo and Isabella* was crowded with no fewer than 13 carefully rendered figures; *Rienzi* lavished loving care on the armor of the 14th Century Roman adventurer who was the hero of Bulwer-Lytton's novel; in Rossetti's painting, the figure of the Virgin was surrounded with an elaborately precise emerald-green vine. A few weeks before the Academy deadline for exhibitors, Rossetti secretly submitted his work to a less prestigious London art show, the Free Exhibition at Hyde Park Corner, leaving Millais and Hunt to wonder why their Brother had deserted them on the eve of battle. He never gave them a reason and even avoided them for a time. As it happened, *Mary Virgin* was well reviewed by several critics, the entries of Hunt and Millais were cordially received at the Academy, and all three works found buyers. Yet in a way the Brothers felt let down. They had hoped to jolt officialdom, and nobody even bothered to ask what the initials P.R.B. meant.

The story was very different the following year. At the Academy exhibition of 1850 Millais weighed in with a couple of entries, including *Ferdinand Lured by Ariel*, a work inspired by Shakespeare's *The Tempest* and marked by bright-green color and minute rendering of the

The decorating firm William Morris founded in 1861 spread Pre-Raphaelite concepts to middle-class homes through such everyday means as designs for books and wallpaper. Naturalistic patterns such as Daisy *(above)* replaced richly tapestried walls. Books, Morris maintained, should please the eye as well as the mind; he started a typographical revolution with his Golden Type *(below)*, based on a 15th Century model, and widely spaced on the printed page.

foliage. Hunt entered a wildly imaginative and boldly lighted canvas entitled *A Converted British Family Sheltering a Christian Missionary from the Persecution of the Druids.* The most unconventional entry of all was Rossetti's *Ecce Ancilla Domini (Behold the Handmaiden of the Lord)*, a study of the Annunciation. In traditional treatments of the subject, a graceful arcade is the setting in which the angel appears to Mary; the Virgin herself is beatific, and clad in flowing draperies. Rossetti's Virgin is bemused, dressed in a simple robe, her auburn hair falling straight. Her room is plain, her pallet simple. *Ecce*, Rossetti seems to be saying, "truth to nature."

Apparently less than usually watchful, the Academy jury accepted the paintings of the Brothers. But the secret leaked out about the meaning of P.R.B. and the concepts behind it, and London reviewers construed the movement as nothing less than artistic treason. They accused the Brothers not only of defaming the sublime Raphael but, by implication, the masters who had followed him. Painters before Raphael! Who were they? If the Brothers had their way, the critics argued, art would regress to crude primitivism.

The most reviled of all the Brothers' efforts was another Millais entry, a painting of Christ as a child in Joseph's carpenter shop *(pages 70–71)*. Millais had intended it to be a reverent but realistic study of the Holy Family; to Victorian eyes the painting was a disgraceful display of "deformities, such as the frost-bitten toes of Joseph, the sore heel of the Virgin." Among the attacks, the most virulent came from none other than Charles Dickens, who wrote that Millais' Virgin "would stand out from the rest of the company as a monster in the vilest cabaret in France or the lowest gin-shop in England."

Only a strong counterattack could ward off total calamity for the Brotherhood. Through a mutual friend Millais enlisted support from the formidable John Ruskin. The recent success of Ruskin's *Modern Painters* had made him a force to be reckoned with in the art world. Sublimely confident of his own judgments, he had put his imprimatur on the medieval artists the Pre-Raphaelites admired and had, moreover, preached the gospel of truth to nature. "Go to nature . . . ," Ruskin had written, "selecting nothing, rejecting nothing."

Predictably, he was flattered to learn that the Pre-Raphaelites were heeding his counsel and happy to go to the defense of their Academy entries. He tore off a lengthy letter to *The Times* asserting that "as studies . . . of every minor detail, there has been nothing in art so earnest or so complete as these pictures since the days of Albert Dürer."

With such a champion, the fortunes of the Brotherhood began to improve. Gradually other critics began to see merit in the Pre-Raphaelites. They, in turn, thrived on the new-found applause. The old secret cabal of the Brotherhood went public. Exuberantly extending their credo to the literary sphere, the Brothers wrote poetry and essays and published a magazine they entitled *The Germ*, for its asserted role as an embryo of the arts. And, of course, they went on painting. Since professional models were costly (a shilling an hour) they used friends or posed for one another. Rossetti's sister Christine—later a celebrated poet in her own right—served both as the Virgin Mary for her brother and as Christ for Hunt, which must have made her feel versatile indeed. Another amiable model was the girl Rossetti fell in love with in 1850, Elizabeth Siddal, a redheaded milliner who became the Pre-Raphaelites' ideal of female beauty.

Eventually the Brotherhood's busy utopia of high art and fraternal high jinks broke up—an inevitable outcome, perhaps, of maturing spirits and popular favor. Millais' was the most spectacular defection. In 1854 he was elected an Associate of the Royal Academy and began a swift rise to respectability and fame. So thoroughly did he embrace artistic convention that in time he felt no compunction whatever about painting a picture called *Bubbles* that served as advertising for Pears' soap, or about pontificating to his old comrade Hunt: "You take my advice, old boy, and just take the world as it is, and don't make it your business to rub people the wrong way."

In the same year that Millais was tapped by the Academy, Hunt decided to devote himself to religious art, and embarked on the first of three trips to the Holy Land; he alone of the Brotherhood's original founders would continue to preserve its principles in paint. Rossetti did not hold the fort in London for very long. More and more he turned to poetry, and his paintings—mostly of melancholy-faced women—acquired a stylized look in which symbolism and ornamental patterns gradually eclipsed the search for simple truth.

In later years Rossetti laughed off the P.R.B. as "the visionary vanities of half a dozen boys." But he was selling his Brothers short. Short-lived as it was, the P.R.B. made a singular contribution to English art. In truth, it was an avant-garde movement, English-style. In consulting the past, the Pre-Raphaelites were not fleeing the present but seeking ways to sharpen their vision. Their detailed portraits of sticks, stones, clouds and daffodils were little hymns to creation—Wordsworth without words—and their vivid, gemlike colors were paeans to the rainbow. There is no denying that the work of the P.R.B. was sometimes cloying and empty. But at its best it achieved a marvelous poetic fervor, a brightness beside which traditional British painting dimmed.

After the Brothers separated, their influence continued, although perhaps not as they expected. Their art introduced a decorative vocabulary of floral forms and fresh colors that even inspired designers of household goods, furniture and textiles. Probably the best known of these artist-decorators was the versatile William Morris. Sharing the Pre-Raphaelites' passion for the medieval, reacting as they did against the shoddiness of the mass-produced wares of the Industrial Revolution, Morris in 1861 formed a company for the manufacture of utilitarian articles designed by first-rate artists. Whether the article was a table or a bed, a jug or a candlestick, Morris was determined that every one of them represent honest craftsmanship, honest value, honest function; so eager was he to mix ethics with esthetics that one might say every Morris cream pitcher wore a halo.

The Pre-Raphaelites' influence extended even further. Their curling linear intricacies turned up in the decorative Art Nouveau style

The Morris chair *(above)*, defined in today's dictionaries as "an easy chair with adjustable back and removable cushion," was a major success of William Morris' decorating company. Although Morris' name became part of the language because of it, the chair was actually adapted by an associate, the architect Philip Webb, from a sturdy English provincial type.

WILLIAM MORRIS GALLERY, WALTHAMSTOW

that flourished in Paris and elsewhere at the turn of the century. And much of their artistic fervor rubbed off on Whistler.

When Whistler and Rossetti became neighbors in Chelsea, the district had a fascinating ambiguity. Stretching along the north bank of the Thames, it offered either bourgeois respectability or bohemian permissiveness. Some of Chelsea's houses were very fine indeed, and some very old; Rossetti lived in a mansion that Queen Elizabeth had reputedly lived in as a child.

This was only part of Chelsea's charm, however. Along the shores of the river were boatyards, jetties and taverns. On the opposite bank were unspoiled woods, now the Battersea Park area. A short ride beyond Chelsea was a resort called Cremorne Gardens, with dance halls, peep shows, and a Chinese-style pagoda, where fireworks fizzed at night and the squeals of excited trollops echoed over the river.

In 1863, a year after his wife, Lizzie, died, Dante Gabriel Rossetti *(right)* posed for this photograph with John Ruskin, the cranky, didactic critic who first championed Pre-Raphaelitism, the artistic movement Rossetti helped to found. Grief, time, success and self-indulgence were eroding the 35-year-old Rossetti's once-devastating good looks. His lard-padded features and balding brow now seemed more appropriate for a comfortable merchant than for an esthetic revolutionary.

By now Rossetti had suffered a deep personal tragedy. He and Elizabeth Siddal had lived together since 1850 in close domestic harmony; then it became apparent that she was suffering from tuberculosis. In 1860 Rossetti married her—at Ruskin's urging—in the hope that a legal alliance might prove therapeutic. It was not; nor was anything else. She gave birth to a stillborn child, and took to easing her pains with laudanum. Two years later she died of an overdose of drugs reported as "accidental," but rumors of suicide persisted. Engulfed by grief, Rossetti placed the only manuscript he had of his poems in her coffin, between her cold cheek and red hair.

Thereafter, Rossetti veered between moods of morbid seclusion—abetted by drugs—and fits of wild hilarity in the company of his Chelsea entourage. Rossetti's mansion had been remodeled to accommodate four residents, providing each with a bedroom, a small study and the use of studio space; meals were taken communally. At this time the three occupants besides Rossetti were his brother, William, the young novelist George Meredith, and the poet Algernon Charles Swinburne. The arrangement was lively, if not always congenial. Meredith was a fresh-air enthusiast who kept trying to drag Rossetti out for jogs along the Thames. Swinburne and an effete artist friend, Simeon Solomon, loved to strip naked and whoop from room to room. Homosexual frolicking was not Swinburne's only diversion; he also enjoyed flagellation and the writings of the Marquis de Sade.

Almost as interesting as Rossetti's housemates were the animals in the back yard. Rossetti fancied himself a zookeeper, and at various times his menagerie included monkeys, armadillos, gazelles, peacocks, a kangaroo, a wombat and a large black bull with which its owner liked to converse. Still, Rossetti was not entirely satisfied; he especially yearned for an elephant. He planned to teach it to wash windows, with a sponge in its trunk, so that people would ask who owned such a smart elephant and then come and buy his pictures.

During the tenancy of the wombat, an occasional caller at the house was the Reverend Charles Dodgson, later famous as Lewis Carroll. The wombat used to fall asleep on the table and one night after dinner crawled into a cigar box just before somebody closed the lid. It was found months later, a skeleton, but it did not pass into oblivion. Dodgson appears to have converted it into the torpid dormouse of the Mad Tea Party in *Alice's Adventures in Wonderland,* and indeed adapted the whole tone of that celebrated affair from a Rossetti dinner. (Years later, after dosings of chloral and liquor had wreaked havoc with Rossetti, he tormented himself by imagining that Carroll's nonsense poem *The Hunting of the Snark,* once described as "the impossible voyage of an improbable crew to find an inconceivable creature," was a vicious satire on himself and the Pre-Raphaelites.)

A more welcome guest at Rossetti's table was a remarkable scamp named Charles Augustus Howell. Both Rossetti and Whistler delighted in him. The son of an English drawing master teaching in Portugual, Howell had been caught cheating at cards and had been shipped home by his father. In London he attached himself to artistic people. Hired by John Ruskin as a secretary, Howell more than once pocketed funds Ruskin gave him to pass on to some poor artist. He also won the trust of Swinburne, then turned blackmailer and threatened to sell the indiscreet letters Swinburne had written to him. Howell could, however, be useful to artists, talking dealers into buying their works, bargaining for better prices and inventing new projects for them. One day in Chelsea when Whistler was broke, he saw Howell strutting by his window. Whistler complained of his straits. Howell pointed out that the artist must have a gold mine locked up in the plates of his etchings of the Thames and *The French Set.* Why not take fresh impressions and sell them? When Whistler replied that his press was broken, Howell strode into the house. In no time he had repaired the press and soon restored Whistler to solvency by selling off the new prints.

Eventually Howell was to perform an unusual service for Rossetti as well. He persuaded Rossetti to exhume the poems he had buried in his wife's coffin. Howell supervised all the grim details and recovered the moldy packet in its calfskin cover. After a doctor had disinfected and dried every page, the verses were returned to Rossetti. They were then published—and cordially received. Buoyed by his success, the poet began, after the fallow years, to write again. For Rossetti it was virtually a resurrection, courtesy of Charles Augustus Howell.

For all the fascinations of Chelsea, Whistler in the early 1860s was far from contented. Now just past 30, he was in the process of finding himself as an artist—and not at all sure of what he was going to find. He had seen almost too much of the world—the United States, Russia, France, England. He had been exposed to two warring schools of art, the trend toward down-to-earth realism in France and the romanticism set in motion by the Pre-Raphaelites. His natural responsiveness led him to adopt certain characteristics of each. But what was to be his personal form of expression? It was bound, of course, to be an amalgam, but how would he stamp it with his own hallmark? Unsure of his objectives, he wrote his friend Fantin-Latour in Paris: "I am horribly depressed at the moment. It's always the same—work that's so hard and uncertain. I am *so slow.* When will I achieve a more rapid way of painting? . . . Oh, Fantin, I know so little."

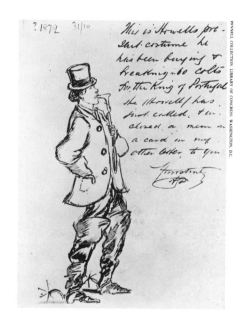

The bubbling high spirits of the artists of Chelsea in the 1870s are reflected in this pen-and-ink sketch of Charles Augustus Howell by Henry Dunn, one of Dante Gabriel Rossetti's entourage. Howell, a rogue much beloved by the Chelsea art circle, had told Rossetti that he was keeping himself in funds by buying horses for the King of Portugal. Rossetti found this claim wildly hilarious, and Dunn escalated the amusement by picturing Howell as a high-booted horseman, with the added note that Howell "has been buying and breaking in 60 colts for the King."

The Pre-Raphaelite Rebels

In the autumn of 1848 three young painters bent on reforming English art banded together with four recruits (two more painters, a sculptor and a writer) in a secret society. The three—Dante Gabriel Rossetti, 20; William Holman Hunt, 21; and John Everett Millais, 19—named their group the Pre-Raphaelite Brotherhood (P.R.B. for short) and vowed to recapture the honesty and simplicity that they found lacking in current British painting, but which they saw in abundance in Italian painting before the 16th Century and the reign of Raphael.

The Brothers believed that the artist must observe a scrupulous fidelity to nature. If he painted an outdoor scene he should use the bright colors of the real countryside, and render every leaf with botanical accuracy. If he painted the Holy Family he should make them look like the poor people they actually were. His subject should be a serious one: if he drew on literature, he should choose a significant moment from an important work; or if he turned to contemporary themes, he should show an awareness of social problems—those, for example, of the new industrial proletariat.

Above all, the P.R.B. credo asserted, the artist must present his personal vision with total integrity. In seeking this goal the Brothers struck off on divergent paths, and by 1854 the group had disintegrated. But its gift to the Victorian world was the moving idealism of its members and the indisputable beauty of some of their works.

Diligently pursuing the P.R.B. principle of truth to nature, Rossetti spent three weeks in the wind and rain, shielded by an "umbrella tied over my head to my buttonhole," painting the autumn background of *The Bower Meadow*. In this mistily romantic re-creation of medieval womanhood, all of the languidly erotic female figures are based on Rossetti's mistress and later wife, Elizabeth Siddal, but were painted into the picture 10 years after her tragic death.

Dante Gabriel Rossetti:
The Bower Meadow, 1872

69

William Holman Hunt: *The Scapegoat*, 1854

Dante Gabriel Rossetti: *The Girlhood of Mary Virgin*, 1849

The Pre-Raphaelites painted religious pictures with such realism that many Victorians were offended. Critics especially disliked the plebeian look of Millais' *Christ in the House of His Parents (above, right)*. In it Mary kneels to comfort her child as He holds up His hand, which has been gashed by a nail; Joseph leans over to examine the wound as St. Anne and his assistant watch solicitously; young John the Baptist brings water, and sheep waiting to be fed outside the door complete the homely scene. Millais went to great pains to ensure an effect of naturalism. He actually painted the picture in a London carpenter's shop, sleeping there each night to absorb its atmosphere. The carpenter himself posed for Joseph's figure and the artist's father was the model for the face.

The Brothers often used family and friends as models. In Rossetti's *The Girlhood of Mary Virgin*

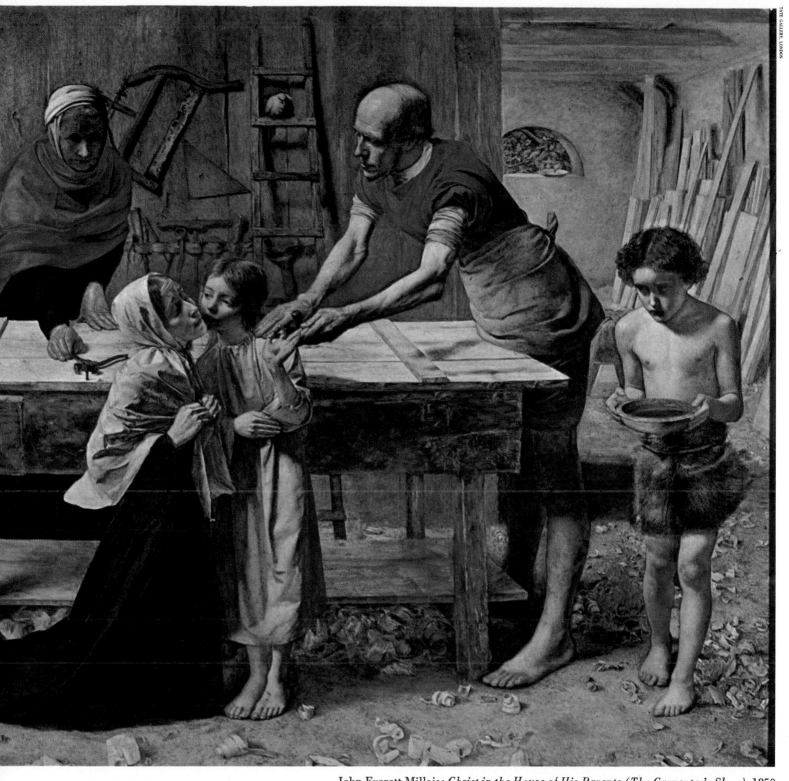

John Everett Millais: *Christ in the House of His Parents (The Carpenter's Shop)*, 1850

(bottom, left), the quiet faces of Mary and St. Anne are those of his sister and mother, and the background figure of Mary's father, St. Joachim, is that of a local London handy man. Rossetti felt that conventional treatments of the theme of the Virgin's education, showing her learning to read, were "incompatible with those times," so he painted her instead learning to embroider; she copies a lily held by a young angel.

Pursuing his own ideas of authenticity, Holman Hunt went all the way to Palestine to do his research for *The Scapegoat (top, left)*. He painted this work on the salt flats by the Dead Sea, a gun beside his easel to protect him against robbers. With a red cloth tied around its horns to signify wickedness, the goat represents an annual ritual of the ancient Hebrews in which the animal was driven into the desert in symbolic atonement for man's sins.

71

Sir Edward Coley Burne-Jones: *The Baleful Head*, 1884-1888

In addition to the Bible, classical and medieval legends inspired many Pre-Raphaelite canvases. *The Baleful Head (above)*, by the leader of a second generation of P.R.B.-influenced artists, Edward Burne-Jones, is based on a version of the Perseus story written by the versatile painter-author-designer William Morris. Perseus was a hero of Greek mythology who rescued, wooed and won the maiden Andromeda. Here he gives her a glimpse of his prize trophy, the head of the terrible gorgon Medusa. She gazes timidly at its reflection in a pool, for to look at it directly would make her turn to stone.

Holman Hunt's *The Lady of Shalott (right)* illustrates Alfred Lord Tennyson's poetic rendition of an Arthurian legend. The Lady sits weaving a tapestry of the world as it is reflected in her mirror. Although forbidden to neglect her work and look out the window, she yields to temptation to watch the handsome Lancelot ride by; the mirror cracks and the thread flies out of the loom to entangle her —signifying the fatal curse she has brought on herself. Hunt's painting, intended as a sermon against disobedience and dereliction of duty, underscores the message with symbolic background figures of the Virgin praying for her child *(left)* and Hercules performing one of his labors *(right)*.

William Holman Hunt: *The Lady of Shalott*, 1886-1905

An allegory called *Work* by Rossetti's teacher, Ford Madox Brown—not a member of the P.R.B., but a close friend—illustrates the strong social consciousness of the Pre-Raphaelites. Based on the philosopher Thomas Carlyle's maxim that "all true work is Religion," it pays tribute to those who toil, with their hands or their minds. Carlyle himself is to the right of the central group of street laborers, glancing at the viewer. He stands with F. D. Maurice, a benefactor of the working class; the two men symbolize "brainworkers." On the road behind them cluster the unemployed, a few of whom have found short-term jobs carrying sandwich boards in a political campaign. The idle rich sit on horseback behind the excavation. A tattered flower vendor *(left)* and ragged children in the foreground are victims of society's failure to provide education and employment. In a sonnet he wrote about *Work*, Brown chided the fashionable lady ("Ah, beauteous tripping dame with bell-like skirts") under the blue parasol for lavishing care on her "scarlet-coated hound" *(left, foreground)* instead of on the abandoned waifs.

74

Ford Madox Brown: *Work*, 1852-1865

IV

Whistler's Mother

On a brief trip to South America, Whistler painted several fine pictures of the sea. Among them is this shimmering view of Valparaiso's harbor, dotted with specks of paint representing distant lights. The first full night scene that Whistler painted, this is one of the impressionistic works that he later called a Nocturne.

Nocturne in Blue and Gold: Valparaiso, 1866

Toward the end of 1863 Anna Mathilda Whistler crossed the Atlantic to share her son's house in London. She was now 56, failing in sight and generally frail in health. She had not seen her darling Jimmy for almost a decade, and longed to be near him and her stepdaughter, Deborah. Moreover, life in the United States, at this time of civil war, had begun to be uncomfortable for her; despite her long residence in Connecticut, her sympathies lay with the South, where she had lived as a girl, and where her younger son, William, was now on active duty as a doctor with the Army of the Confederacy.

One marvels at this prim, quiet woman, who is known chiefly as the mother image of the American nation, yet whose destiny drove her into unlikely environments, from Czarist St. Petersburg to bohemian Chelsea. She re-entered her firstborn's life at a critical stage in his development. Buoyed by his triumph at the Salon des Refusés in Paris, he was nevertheless unsure of his identity as an artist, aware of his shortcomings, trying one idea after another. Serious tensions were to beset him, and manifest themselves in violent, sometimes irrational outbursts. If Anna Whistler disapproved of his antics, there is no hint of it in the lengthy letters she wrote to relatives and friends back home. Perhaps, with pristine innocence, she simply remained blind to Whistler's darker side. But certainly she was full of admiration for his talent, unbounded in her faith in him.

Whistler returned his mother's love. However ignobly he might behave toward others, he treated her with unfailing deference. True, he did not encourage her presence in the studio part of the house at No. 7 Lindsey Row, and when he took her to church on Sundays he left her at the door. But he also showed her off to his friends and patrons. She was charmed with the wife and daughters of Michael Spartali, the Greek consul general in London, and she journeyed with Whistler to Liverpool for a stay at the estate of Frederick Leyland, a rich shipowner for whom Whistler produced some family portraits. When health did not permit her to travel or dine out, she found no less pleasure in her son's at homes and his lively Chelsea friends, notably the effete and dissolute

Overstuffed chairs fought for space with bric-a-brac in the modish Victorian room advertised by a London furniture store *(right)* and realized *(below)* in the boudoir of Princess Victoria, granddaughter of Queen Victoria and Prince Albert. Though such opulence was fashionable, Whistler decorated his own living quarters with New England simplicity; and in his work he generally shunned excessively cluttered settings or backgrounds.

Swinburne, whose demonic red locks she patted as he sat by her knee.

Installed in her own rooms on an upper floor of the house, Mrs. Whistler thrived in surroundings that were strange for Victorian London. The current preference in decoration called for cozy, cluttered interiors, plush-lined grottoes in which one burrowed against the damp of England's climate. Whistler had defied the fashion in its entirety, combining two beliefs that were increasingly to become central to his art. One was his rising rapport with the Far East, the other his growing conviction that art should not stop at the picture frame, but should encompass the very environment in which one lived.

The inside of No. 7 Lindsey Row was airy, almost empty. Plain matting covered the floors, furniture was limited to essential pieces, and walls were kept mostly unadorned. The effect was not unlike that of the austere New England houses Whistler had known as a child—he once said that in most houses he liked the pantry best because of its bare whitewashed look. Yet at the same time the effect was also undeniably Oriental. The use of color was sparing but carefully planned, subtly highlighted here and there in a vase or a lacquer box on a shelf, a fan or two tacked to a wall. The same restraint was apparent in Whistler's studio. Painted pale yellow to reflect the light, it was devoid of furnishings except for a straight chair, a bench for the artist's model, a plain gold screen, an easel and a small table that held Whistler's palette like a tea tray. All this was in startling contrast to most artists' working quarters, with their heaps of curios, antique casts, weapons, armor, brocades, everything to impress visitors and bear witness that the occupant was a worthy fellow and a formidable connoisseur.

Whistler's acquisition of Orientalia, begun on visits to Paris at a new shop called La Porte Japonaise and later augmented by purchases from a dealer in Amsterdam, consisted mainly of fans, woodcuts, and blue-and-white porcelains. Mrs. Whistler took note of her son's new predilection, and its effect on his work, in a letter in 1864 to a friend back home. "Are you interested in old china?" she wrote. "This artistic abode of my son is ornamented by a very rare collection of Japanese and Chinese. He considers the paintings upon them the finest specimens of art, and his companions (artists), who resort here for an evening's relaxation occasionally, get enthusiastic as they handle and examine the curious figures portrayed. . . . You will not wonder that [his] inspiration should be . . . of the same cast. He is finishing at his studio a very beautiful picture for which he is to be paid one hundred guineas without the frame, that is always separate. I'll try to describe this inspiration to you. A girl seated, as if intent upon painting a beautiful jar which she rests upon her lap—a quiet and easy attitude."

Mrs. Whistler went on to describe the portrait now known as *Purple and Rose: The Lange Lijzen of the Six Marks (page 93)*. The first part of the title represents the colors Whistler chose to accent. The *"lange lijzen"*—Dutch for "long Elizas"—refers to the tall, lissome girls immobilized on the vase the model is holding, a type of late-17th Century Chinese pottery, and the "six marks" to the means by which the potter identified his handiwork. The painting itself is almost as complicated as the title, rather cluttered with Oriental artifacts, mindful almost of a curio shop. Whistler was soon to do much better in emulating the spare, sensitively suggestive work of accomplished Eastern artists.

What is perhaps more interesting about this work is that the model Mrs. Whistler described was very likely her son's mistress, Jo Heffernan. Whether she knew—or suspected—the extent of their relationship can only be conjectured. A stern Presbyterian, she could not have reacted happily to the prospect of Jo's continued presence in the household. In any event the matter was resolved by Jo's moving out, possibly around the time of Mrs. Whistler's letter, for in it there is a thinly disguised note of satisfaction. "God answered my prayers for his welfare, by leading me here," she wrote of her son. "All those most truly interested in him remark upon the improvement in his home and health. The dear fellow studies as far as he can my comforts, as I do all his interests, practically—it is so much better for him generally to spend his evenings tête-à-tête with me, tho I do not interfere with hospitality in a rational way, but I do all I can to render his home as his father's was." Her roles as wife and mother appeared to be merging.

Whistler, however, had a mind of his own. Despite Jo's departure from the house the lovers remained close for another half-dozen years, and he continued to rely on her as a model. He painted two more portraits of her in the same year as *Purple and Rose*. In the enchanting *Symphony in White No. 2: The Little White Girl (page 89)*, Jo, dressed in white, holds a Japanese fan; on the mantel behind her is a blue vase. Her wistful expression is reflected in a mirror. The effect is one of tranquillity and balance. Swinburne was moved to write a poem in praise of the picture, and the Royal Academy accepted it for exhibition. But Whistler had not yet absorbed the essence of Far Eastern art. Its influence in the painting is still mainly a matter of superficial trimmings, a whiff of cherry blossoms in a Victorian parlor.

His *Caprice in Purple and Gold No. 2: The Golden Screen (pages 92-93)* also features the trimmings—Jo's kimono, the gold screen, the

"Before the Mirror: Verses under a Picture" was written by poet Algernon Charles Swinburne after he saw Whistler's *The Little White Girl (page 89)*. Whistler so admired the poem that he had it printed on gold paper and pasted to the frame of the painting. Below are verses four through six.

"Come snow, come wind or thunder
High up in air,
I watch my face, and wonder
At my bright hair;
Nought else exalts or grieves
The rose at heart, that heaves
With love of her own leaves and lips
*   that pair.*

"She knows not loves that kiss'd her
She knows not where.
Art thou the ghost, my sister,
White sister there,
Am I the ghost, who knows?
My hand, a fallen rose,
Lies snow-white on white snows, and
*   takes no care.*

"I cannot see what pleasures
Or what pains were;
What pale new loves and treasures
New years will bear;
What beam will fall, what shower,
What grief or joy for dower;
But one thing knows the flower; the
*   flower is fair."*

---

spindling black chair suggesting a rhythm of ebony chopsticks. But Whistler's arrangement of the elements of the composition, the flat planes and angular patterns, achieves an effect more basically Eastern than had his earlier attempts. The design approached the boldness and sharpness of the Japanese prints shown strewn on the rug.

Whistler was learning, slowly, to do what the Eastern artist so often did: to stand off from his work, to select his material with an objective eye, and to arrange it consciously and sensitively. The approach was a congenial one for him, fortifying his own artistic impulses, and his growing mastery of it gave him the confidence to seek a commission that would allow the full expression of his new style. He found a willing patron in his Greek friend, Consul General Spartali, and a dazzling subject, the younger of Spartali's two daughters, Christine. It is easy to imagine the ancient Greeks setting off to rescue *her* from Troy; she had glorious black hair, dark, liquid eyes and ivory skin.

Whistler prepared a Japanese setting in his studio and Christine, accompanied by her sister, came regularly to pose in a Japanese robe, her long hair hanging loose. The sessions went well at first; Whistler would work from about 10 until after 2, when his mother would serve lunch. For these repasts Mrs. Whistler seems to have exercised considerable culinary imagination; on one day the menu included pheasant and champagne, on another raw tomatoes and canned apricots with cream.

Whether from indigestion or fatigue, Christine fell ill and the portrait was delayed. There was more trouble to come. When at last the picture was finished, Christine and her sister loved it, but their father did not. It is hard for modern viewers to understand why. *La Princesse du Pays de la Porcelaine (The Princess from the Land of Porcelain, page 118)* is a rich but delicate harmony of color, cool pewter against warm amber. In the striking contrasts of color, Christine's dark Mediterranean beauty might have been lost, yet it emerges to dominate the canvas decisively. Evidently all that Consul General Spartali could see was that his little Hellenic beauty had been rigged up as a Japanese doll, and he refused to buy the portrait.

In Whistler's discomfited state, his sympathetic neighbor Dante Gabriel Rossetti offered to display the picture in his own studio to try to attract another purchaser. For a considerable period it had no takers. But while *La Princesse* hung in Rossetti's studio it produced one unexpected benefit. One of the prospective collectors who rejected it did so because of the flamboyant signature scrawled across the top of the canvas. Rossetti then suggested that Whistler henceforth sign his works more discreetly, with a symbol or trademark like the P.R.B. initials once used by the members of the Pre-Raphaelite Brotherhood. Rising to this idea, Whistler applied his imagination to the initials of his name, and from the shape of the letters "J.M.W." evolved his now-famous butterfly insignia. No one knows on which of his works it first appeared; after the butterfly became popular, owners of his early paintings frequently asked him to add it to these canvases. Whistler himself prized the device because it resembled the ideographs that often appeared on Oriental paintings to indicate the identity of the var-

Chinese porcelain, such as the 17th Century K'ang Hsi plates above and below, became popular in the 1860s. Whistler helped introduce fine china to British collectors. His appreciation for the graceful plates and vases shows in a sketch *(left)* drawn for a catalogue illustrating a private collection.

ious purchasers. And with his increasingly keen sense of design, he often placed the butterfly so that it added an essential element of decoration to his compositions.

In the summer of 1865 Whistler took a two-month vacation with Jo at Trouville, on the Normandy coast. It was a good time to leave. The Spartali affair had been unsettling, and conveniently Whistler's brother, William, had just arrived in London to establish a practice and was available to keep a watchful eye on Mrs. Whistler. The stay at the French seaside resort provided a welcome change for Whistler. His old friend Courbet was there, painting, and so were Monet and Charles François Daubigny. In the evening Jo entertained the group with Irish songs, and feasts of shrimp salad were followed by midnight dips in the bracing sea. Whistler seemed to be completely relaxed. Occasionally he would take up his brush. In one of the paintings he produced, *Harmony in Blue and Silver: Trouville,* he surrendered himself to space, to uncluttered expanses of sea, sand and sky. It is a sky streaked with cloud, but sparingly; the Japanese were teaching Whistler the eloquence of economy.

He was also using touches of impasto to produce a thick surface texture in some compositions. This technique suggests yet another of the debts he owed to Courbet, but while the two men were together at Trouville Whistler was apparently entertaining some far from grateful thoughts about his French mentor and his style. He later expressed them in a letter to his colleague of the early days in Paris, Fantin-Latour. "Courbet and his influence was disgusting . . . all that he represented was bad for me . . . this damned Realism made an immediate appeal to my vanity as a painter . . . 'Long live Nature' . . . that cry, *mon cher*, was the greatest misfortune for me. . . . Ah! if only I had been a pupil of Ingres. I don't say that out of any rhapsodical enthusiasm for his pictures; I like them half-heartedly. . . . I feel that one has much further to go and much more beautiful things to paint. But I repeat—if only I had been his pupil; what a master he would have proved, and how he would have healthily led us."

The letter comes through as a cry of anguish. Manifestly the Trouville stay was not the idyllic interlude it appeared to be. Whistler, in fact, was undergoing a major crisis in his art. For all his seeming bravado, he was far from confident about his powers as a painter, unsure of the direction he should take. In his student days in Paris he had admired, even revered, Courbet. But since then he had been exposed to the delicate and abstract qualities of Eastern art. He experienced a strong revulsion against the Frenchman's realism, his raw, heavy modeling of form, his down-to-earth definition of painting as a "completely physical language based on objects instead of words." Other young painters were to share this revulsion and were to abandon the prose of Courbet's realism for the poetry of their own vision, with profound effect on the later course of 19th Century art. For his part, Whistler may have sensed that he, too, would eventually take this road, but self-doubt held him back. In invoking the art of Ingres—with its elegance, its ability to speak volumes in a single, masterful line—he seemed to be seeking a halfway house en route.

Whistler's repudiation of Courbet was so violent that the psychological implications merit notice. Was he wishing he had a stronger master, a leader—or a father? The question cannot be answered. Plainly, however, Whistler's difficulties were personal as well as professional, and soon after his return from Trouville to London they erupted publicly.

In February 1866—forsaking his mother, Jo and the comforts of life in London—Whistler abruptly and mystifyingly took ship for South America. His mission, he said, was to assist Peru and Chile in a war they were waging against Spain; the Spaniards had dispatched a naval squadron into the Pacific to chastise both former colonies. But it is by no means clear that Whistler knew what the fracas was all about. In later years he tried to explain: "There were South Americans to be helped against the Spaniards. Some of these people came to me, as a West Point man, and asked me to join—and it was all done in an afternoon. I was off at once."

He may have engaged in a knight-errant's quest, or in an attempt to

Proudly wearing the uniform of the Confederacy, Dr. William Whistler, the artist's brother, had his picture taken shortly before the end of the Civil War. He was dispatched on a mission to England in early 1865, but the South surrendered while he was still in London and Dr. Whistler remained to establish a surgical practice. In 1877 he married Helen Ionides, the daughter of one of James's earliest patrons.

prove his manhood, or both. In any case the adventure, one of the more enigmatic episodes in his life, lasted nine months. Before British, French and American intervention ended the conflict, Whistler had his only taste of combat when the Spanish fleet bombarded Valparaiso. According to him he led the retreat of Chilean forces from the capital: "The riding was splendid and I, as a West Point man, was head of the procession."

On the voyage home from Valparaiso, Whistler became annoyed at the manner of a fellow passenger, a Haitian Negro, and booted him across the deck and down a companionway. As a result the ship's captain confined Whistler to his quarters. Hearing about it later, William Rossetti upheld the captain, telling Whistler "your conduct was scandalous." William's brother, Dante Gabriel, took the incident more lightly, in this verse:

> *There's a combative Artist named Whistler*
> *Who is, like his own hog-hairs, a bristler:*
> *A tube of white lead*
> *And a punch on the head*
> *Offer varied attractions to Whistler.*

The barb was apt—Whistler was still bristling when he arrived in London, and for reasons wholly obscure knocked down a total stranger in Waterloo Station.

His attack on the Negro aboard ship was perhaps easier to explain. Whistler may have worked himself into a rage over news of the Confederate defeat in the American Civil War the year before; not only was his mother a Southern sympathizer and his brother a former Confederate officer, but his own cadet days at West Point had been spent under the superintendency of none other than Robert E. Lee. Or perhaps Whistler's failure to cut a heroic figure in South America had goaded him to violence. At any rate, although he had once scorned the physical fitness campaigns of his student cronies in Paris, now, at 32, he took up boxing lessons.

He was soon embroiled in another fight—this time with his own brother-in-law. Their relationship had long since soured, primarily because of Jo Heffernan. Although Haden had amicably joined her and Whistler on sketching expeditions, he had refused—on grounds of social propriety—to bring his wife to dine at Whistler's house as long as Jo remained in residence. Even after she departed, Haden would not bring Deborah to dine with her stepmother in a house that had once been polluted by Jo's presence. Whistler was infuriated at the implication that his mother lived in a house unfit for his stepsister to visit. For a while, apparently, he said nothing to Haden about the matter, but it continued to rankle.

In the spring of 1867 Whistler went to Paris to see an exhibition of paintings. One day, as he walked through a narrow street, a workman accidentally spilled some wet plaster on him. Using his new boxing skills, Whistler flattened the man and was taken before a magistrate; he claimed the protection of the American Minister and was released.

A few days later he happened to meet Haden, also in Paris for the exhibition, and without a word of warning slammed him through a plate-glass shop window. He was taken before the same magistrate and this time was compelled to pay a fine.

Back in London Haden rushed to the Burlington Fine Arts Club, to which both he and Whistler belonged, and threatened to resign unless Whistler was expelled. Haden was a highly successful member of the Establishment and Whistler certainly was not. The Club duly ousted him. Out of friendship the two Rossetti brothers departed with him. Whistler and Haden never again spoke to one another, and Deborah was able to see her dear Jimmy only by stealth.

Whistler's outbursts, his uncontrolled combativeness, were symptomatic of deepening conflicts. One stemmed from the fact that he was not really at ease in his adopted environment. He could not find his niche in it. He admired London's upper crust and hung about its fringes, yet scorned it. On the other hand, the bohemian world to which he turned as a relief was at odds with a streak of puritanism within him. His displays of belligerence attracted the attention he craved and evidently built up his self-esteem. But they also drained his emotions and consumed his energies. Behind his arrogance was uncertainty. This was true of him not only as a man but as an artist. He rubbed out many more paintings than he finished.

And yet he kept at his easel, stubbornly, passionately, as if there were no other course conceivable for him to take. For deep within him the conviction persisted that he had something to contribute to the mainstream of art, perhaps not so much in pictures themselves as in a philosophical idea about them. A decade was to pass before he refined this idea into a single, cogent and now-celebrated sentence: "Art should be independent of clap-trap—should stand alone, and appeal to the artistic sense of eye or ear, without confounding this with emotions entirely foreign to it, as devotion, pity, love, patriotism and the like."

In a sense this was simply Whistler's variation on an ancient and honorable theme, summarized as Art for Art's Sake, and since become a well-worn cliché. But many a worthy idea shrivels and dies because it is not quite right for the times in which it is put forth. Whistler happened to articulate his thoughts at a moment of perfect receptivity. The notion that art should serve as the handmaiden of religion, history or mythology was dead. The more recent concept—championed by Courbet—that it should serve as the mirror of everyday realism was dying. Where, then, was art to turn? What was its new subject matter to be? In an age when individualism was insistently on the rise, was a precise representation of a given object less important, perhaps, than the artist's personal, and often abstract, vision of it?

Alert young painters of Whistler's day were churning over these questions, and Whistler's pronouncement pointed to possible answers. His gift for a phrase, his flair for showmanship, no doubt helped publicize his ideas more than parallel views held by other men. But he could not have become a prophet of modern art without the absolute sincerity of his beliefs.

In applying them to his own work Whistler chose as his subject matter some of the basic vocabulary of art itself: color, line, rhythm, tonal harmonies, decorative patterns, deliberate arrangements. These, he felt, were the elements to be emphasized on a canvas; if in so doing he had to play down the exact rendition of a person or object, that, after all, was his prerogative as an artist. Indications of this approach had appeared in the decorative Eastern accents and studied color relationships of his portraits of Jo Heffernan and Christine Spartali, and in the practice he followed of calling his works Arrangements and Harmonies in various colors—a device 20th Century painters would adopt in labeling their efforts with such titles as *White on White* or *Improvisation* or simply *Composition No. 7*.

The trend of Whistler's thinking was still more evident in a series of paintings he produced during—of all times—his bellicose venture to Valparaiso. From his swashbuckling account of this exploit it would not seem that he had had any time to spare for nonmilitary matters. But he did, in fact, paint five scenes of Valparaiso's harbor, and they, rather than any feat of derring-do, were his real achievement on this strange journey. Two of the paintings have since been lost; the survivors, however, amply attest to Whistler's waning interest in realism. His harbor might as easily have been Trouville or Southampton as Valparaiso, or a place that existed only in his eye; the foreground of one scene contains a highly unlikely feature for South American landscapes, a spray of Japanese foliage. There are no authentically identifiable details of the Chilean capital, no picturesque local landmarks. Unlike the Wapping vessels Whistler had pictured in his Thames scenes, the ships lack rigging and seamen; they are not extraneous objects placed upon the water, but are fused with sea and sunlight or twilight. The port of Valparaiso *(page 76)* is arranged to fit not the facts but Whistler's ideas of composition and tonal harmony.

Back in London in the late 1860s, amid his boxing lessons and bouts of truculence, Whistler pressed on toward his artistic goal and in his quest fell in with a curious fellow traveler—a man he later eulogized as "the greatest artist that, in the century, England might have cared for and called her own." Albert Joseph Moore was an obscure painter seven years Whistler's junior, a crotchety recluse who lived in a leaky attic. Superficially, Moore's art seemed to belong to the Neoclassical school of Victorian painting that had produced such Academy heroes as Sir Lawrence Alma-Tadema, Sir Frederick Leighton and Sir Edward John Poynter, one of Whistler's cronies during his student days. These artists had shopped for their subject matter among the myths of ancient Greece and Rome and had been knighted for their pains. But Moore had no discernible interest in antique history and rudely turned his back on the artistic potentialities of Andromache, Psyche and Persephone. His own chief source of inspiration was the Parthenon frieze—not, however, for the story material it offered but for the majestic harmonies of its figures. Thus inspired, Moore created his own horizontal arrangements of figures, mostly seminaked girls sitting or reclining on marble benches; the link with Greece consisted mainly of the girls' classic poses and draperies, which Moore painted with extraordinary skill.

What attracted Whistler was the sheer decorative appeal of Moore's pictures, his perfectly balanced compositions, and, above all, his gift for unexpected and sumptuous color combinations. Moore was so fascinated by color that he would paint the same intricate picture three times just to satisfy himself how it would look in three totally different color versions. Like Whistler, he cared little for orthodox titles, tagging his works with such labels as *Beads*, *Apples* and *Pomegranates*, titles that had almost no connection with their subject matter. All of this endeared him to Whistler, who took him rowing on the Thames, ate with him in cheap cafés and went with him to inspect Greek sculpture at the British Museum.

Spurred by Moore's unyielding estheticism, Whistler took a fling at creating what he called "an ideal style." This interlude was brief, but crucial to his development. One of its more finished products, in 1867, was *Symphony in White No. 3 (pages 98-99)*, a study of two white-robed girls, a theme Moore had painted the year before. It was this work that elicited Whistler's famous retort to a London critic who complained that there were many other colors beside white in the picture: red, brown, blue, yellow: "*Bon Dieu!* Did this wise person expect white hair and chalked faces? And does he then, in his astounding consequence, believe that a symphony in F contains no other note, but shall be a continued repetition of F, F, F? . . . Fool!"

Most of Whistler's "ideal style" works were small sketches in pastel colors or very liquid paint, intended as preliminary studies for large projects that he never consummated. They reveal leftover touches of the Oriental, as well as touches of Moore's pseudo-Greek art; in the female figures Whistler depicted, the Japanese kimono is combined with the Greek chiton in a triumph of eclectic chic. But the real importance of these amalgams lies in their bold air of freedom, as if Whistler had made a sudden breakthrough into a new realm. In a set of sketches he produced and called *Six Projects*, showing clusters of women on balconies and promenades overlooking a summer sea *(pages 96-97)*, the brushwork is exuberant and the colors are delectable. In the same ebullient vein he painted groups of Japanese-type girls on a balustrade over the Thames, with hints of London smokestacks and warehouses on the far shore as if this were the most natural place in the world for East and West to meet.

This interlude of spontaneous sketches and fanciful anomalies served an important purpose for Whistler. It added to his much-needed self-confidence and thus helped him confront the future more on his own terms. Even as he dabbled in these essentially minor efforts, he was also devoting time and energy and thought to a more ambitious work that would, as none other, ensure his lasting fame: the portrait of his mother *(page 114)*.

Exactly when Whistler began it, or what struggles attended its creation, is not known. The sitter herself mentioned it in a chatty letter in 1866 to a friend back in America. Mrs. Whistler noted that some of

The chaotic attic storeroom of the Royal Academy, where rejected works were piled like mass-produced paintings at a discount shop, was the subject of an unknown 19th Century artist's aptly named painting *The Royal Academy— the Hurly Burly (above)*. Whistler's portrait *The Artist's Mother* was stashed in such a room before it was grudgingly exhibited by the Academy in 1872.

her son's "artistic friends" had come to see the portrait: "I was up in my Japanese bedroom seated in my armchair and refused not the particular friends and admirers of my son's work." One of them, she revealed with pardonable maternal pride, had commented: "It has a holy expression. Oh, how much sentiment Whistler has put into his mother's likeness!" The real credit, she felt, belonged to God, "the One source of help on which I rely for the continued success of either of my dear boys."

It was not until 1872 that Whistler submitted the portrait to the Royal Academy's annual exhibition—with dismaying result. The jury gave it a quick brush-off, and it was consigned to a storeroom. But then the venerable Sir William Boxall, whose portrait of Whistler as a young boy had adorned the Academy's walls in 1849, heard of this ignominious outcome and demanded to see the painting. He threatened to resign from the Academy if it were not reconsidered; it was, and was put on exhibit. Whistler still smarted, however, and this was the last time he ever submitted a canvas to the Academy.

By now overfamiliarity has killed the picture for most modern viewers; the mere mention of Whistler's mother tends to produce a horselaugh or suggest a cartoon. But the painting is unarguably a masterpiece. In it Whistler has the best of two artistic worlds: the traditional world of meticulously characterized portraiture and his own newer world in which color and line and pattern and composition are the key elements. There is the same sharp insight into personality that marks the portraits of serene old ladies by Frans Hals. Yet the painting's vertical and horizontal lines, its clean edges and right angles, presage another very different Dutch master, Piet Mondrian, whose simple geometrical arrangements produce a similar masterful effect of balance and repose.

Which of the two worlds preoccupied Whistler more is evident in the way he named his work: *Arrangement in Grey and Black No. 1: The Artist's Mother*. Some time later, defending the first part of this title, he insisted: "Now that is what it is. To me it is interesting as a picture of my mother; but what can or ought the public to care about the identity of the picture?" He did not consider it at all odd to think of his mother in terms of the language of art. When one of his friends joked, "Who would have thought of you having a mother, Jimmy?" he replied, "Yes, indeed I have a mother, and a very pretty bit of color she is, I can tell you."

Mrs. Whistler, as immortalized in her portrait, is a great deal more as well. She is a triumphant symbol. She endows the maternal image with a dignity and plain grace that flatter the whole race of mothers and reassure their offspring. Minding her own business, she does not demand attention or sympathy. She appears self-sufficient, content with her lot. Sitting alone with her feet on a stool, she is as aloof as a Chinese ancestor portrait or a saint in a niche. She will not rise to ring for tea or dust the pictures on the wall. She is outside the stream of life, ready for ritual veneration. As comfortable as she can be on her straight-backed chair, she sits out eternity.

A Search for Simplicity

By the early 1860s Whistler had been painting professionally for nearly 10 years, but he had yet to find a personal style that suited him. With his unusual early facility he had produced a number of genuinely accomplished works, but he was not satisfied. The remainder of the decade was to be a time of trial and experiment, during which he would build upon two existing influences—the realism of Courbet and the romanticism of the Pre-Raphaelites—and add two other, wholly new sources of inspiration: the elegant simplicity of Far Eastern art and the harmonious grace of classical antiquity. It is a measure of his imagination that he took up these apparently unassimilable styles, and a mark of his skill that he succeeded in absorbing what he needed from them to forge a unique, personal idiom.

Whistler's preoccupation with the Orient began with an infatuation for Chinese blue-and-white porcelains, which he collected avidly. Fascinated by their overall decorative pattern, the pure linear mode of drawing and the flat areas of color, he soon began incorporating these elements into his own work. He acquired his love of the antique from a painter friend, Albert Moore, and was especially taken with the graceful lines and calm dignity of a type of sculpture called Tanagra, after the ancient Greek town where it flourished. The arts of East and West, both old and new, were never more felicitously blended than in Whistler's work.

Bridging two of Whistler's styles, this portrait of his mistress Jo Heffernan combines the charm of the Pre-Raphaelites with the delicate beauty of Japan—seen in the fan Jo holds, the vase on the mantel and the blossoms at the lower right. Thus far, the Orient's influence on Whistler was limited to these few touches, but soon it would cause deeper changes in his maturing style.

Symphony in White No. 2: The Little White Girl, 1864

89

A face "languidly contemplative of its own phantom" was the way the poet Algernon Swinburne described the likeness of his friend Whistler's mistress. In this detail of the painting on the preceding page, Jo's beauty is seen as ethereal and fragile, although actually she was robust and voluptuous—the way Courbet painted her. This poetic idealization was a familiar stylistic trait of Dante Gabriel Rossetti and other Pre-Raphaelites with whom Whistler was consorting during the 1860s. But he also drew on an idea long popular in European art. Titian, Rubens, Velázquez and Ingres had all painted women with their reflections in a mirror. Whistler cannot have been unaware that he was matching himself against acknowledged masters in using this device, and he did so with remarkable success.

91

Caprice in Purple and Gold No. 2: The Golden Screen, 1864

Like a child with a new set of toys, Whistler played exuberantly with Oriental paraphernalia in his art before he quieted down and truly assimilated the influence of the East. These two paintings parade all sorts of Chinese and Japanese artifacts in carefree abandon. Robes, hairdos, porcelain, trays and prints assault the eye in a dizzying barrage of patterns, colors and shapes. Whistler has not yet substituted the airy space of a Japanese interior for the clutter of a Victorian parlor.

Overstuffed as they are, however, the paintings emphasize Whistler's obvious skill at handling his materials and his eye for authentic detail. In the painting at the right the model—probably Jo Heffernan—holds a Chinese vase known as "The Lange Lijzen of the Six Marks," respectively

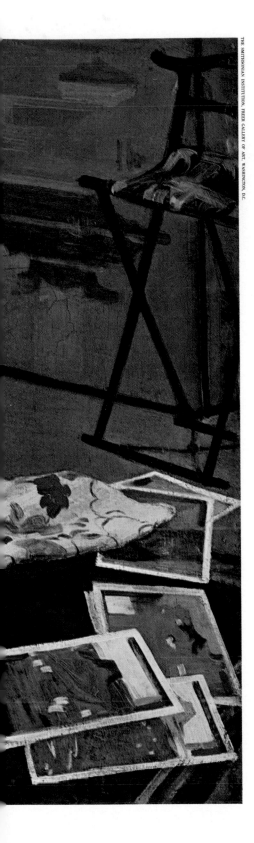

Purple and Rose: The Lange Lijzen of the Six Marks, 1864

referring to the willowy female figures on the base
—literally, "long Elizas" in Dutch—and to the
potter's identifying emblem.

In the painting at left, Jo, clad in a magnificent
silk robe, reclines before a beautifully decorated
screen while examining a Japanese woodcut; other
woodcuts are strewn on the floor. Such prints were
soon to serve Whistler as more than accents;
their contents inspired entire compositions *(next
page)*. Describing his debt to Japan, Whistler later
told his biographers, Joseph and Elizabeth Pennell,
that his idea "was not to go back to the Japanese as
being greater than himself, but to learn what he
could from them . . . and to produce another work
of art: a work founded in tradition no less than
theirs and yet as western as theirs was eastern."

93

Torii Kiyonaga: *Twelve Months in the South*, 1784
"The Fourth Month"

"The Sixth Month"

Among the Japanese woodcuts Whistler owned were two from a series showing life in a geisha house *(above, right)*. He relied heavily on them in the painting at right, in which, for the first time, he moves away from merely showing off Oriental accessories to emulating Japanese *style*. Whistler took the setting—a balcony overlooking the harbor —as well as the languid poses of the figures almost directly from the two woodcuts; even the use of the bamboo blind as a framing device in the upper right corner has been picked up quite literally and adapted as a crucial design element.

While experimenting in the Oriental mode, Whistler also dabbled with the idea of producing pictures on a larger scale than anything he had previously attempted. The sketch at the far right, a view of his studio, was intended as preparation for a picture fully 10 feet high. It was to be a monumental interior scene, including his beautiful mistress Jo Heffernan, a model called "la Japonaise," Whistler himself, and two fellow artists, Fantin-Latour and Albert Moore. Whistler never actually completed the larger work and the plan to include his colleagues also fell through. But the sketch itself, designed and executed very much in the Japanese manner, offers a fascinating and intimate glimpse of the artist at work in his austerely furnished London studio.

Variations in Flesh Color and Green: The Balcony, 1867-1868

The Artist in His Studio, c. 1867-1868

Variations in Blue and Green, c. 1868

Girl with Fan, c. 300 B.C.

Classical art, the fourth great influence on Whistler's style, offered many inspirations, but he particularly concentrated on the delicate beauty of Tanagra figurines, dating from about 300 B.C. These painted terra-cotta sculptures are small—the one above is just over nine inches high—and mostly portray women dressed in flowing draperies and posed informally.

Whistler's version of a Tanagra figurine is seen at the far left in this oil sketch. Its graceful stance and classical garb are in sharp contrast to the other figures, in which Whistler was obviously experimenting with a kind of Oriental brushwork of his own.

With far more subtlety the artist combined the several influences of his recent experience in *Symphony in White No. 3 (overleaf)*. This work shows clear traces of Pre-Raphaelite romanticism, classical harmony and Japanese simplicity. Yet all are fused with a new authority, and the deft interplay of colors and studied arrangement of the elements presage a period in Whistler's art when he would rely much less on others and much more on himself.

97

Symphony in White. No III.- Whistler. 1867-

Symphony in White No. 3, 1867

V

Triumph and Turmoil

During the 1870s Whistler enjoyed the fullest years of his life. As in the '60s, there were some exceedingly odd episodes, and the decade was to end disastrously for him. But it began auspiciously. He acquired a modish new mistress *(opposite)* whose carefully contrived chic complemented his own. Moreover, the critical success of the portrait of his mother attracted other sitters, and he produced, among other works, a series of superb portraits that were as revelatory of character as of his own emerging concepts of art.

The first sitter to find his way to Whistler's studio in the wake of *Mother* was Chelsea's grand old man, the Scottish historian, philosopher and essayist Thomas Carlyle. He had been painted before by George Watts, a popular Victorian artist whose tenebrous Academy-style portrait had not pleased him. Carlyle thought Whistler's portraiture admirable, austere yet sympathetic, and in 1872 he proposed to go through the ordeal of sitting again.

At the first session Carlyle plunked himself down in a chair and ordered, "Fire away." Seeing Whistler bristle at this command, Carlyle added, "If you're fighting battles or painting pictures, the only thing to do is fire away." At the military allusion, Whistler brightened, and began. After many hours of posing and countless rubbings-out of the developing portrait, Carlyle was to dub Whistler "the most absurd creature on the face of the earth," but the two flaming egotists got on well. While the philosopher would chat, the painter would paint, shouting only when his sitter got fidgety, "For God's sake, don't move."

Anxious to get the sessions over with, the irascible Carlyle chided Whistler for using narrow brushes, suggesting he might get the job done faster with larger ones. So Whistler set out some broader brushes, but effectively hidden by the canvas he continued to use the size he preferred. Then his subject was hurt because more time was spent painting his clothing than his features; the face of a great sage should not play second fiddle to an old coat. Then a stand-in had to be recruited when Carlyle finally rebelled at the protracted sittings. But the finished work gratified him, unlike the portrait by Watts, whom he

Whistler never really caught on as a fashionable portraitist because, among other things, he refused to flatter his sitters. He was much more concerned with the purely artistic problems of getting the clothed human figure on canvas in an interesting way. When he exhibited this portrait of his mistress Maud Franklin, one London critic peremptorily dismissed the work as a "vaporous full length" and another sneered at Maud's "curiously shaped" figure.

Arrangement in Black and White No. 1: The Young American, exhibited 1878

had scolded for failing to make his shirt look properly fresh: "Mon, I would have you know that I am in the hobit of wurin' clean linen." Whistler had assuaged the old man by making his collar a spanking white, the brightest spot in the picture *(page 115)*.

Even before the painting was completed, Whistler also began an enchanting portrait of nine-year-old Cicely Alexander, a banker's daughter. One day Carlyle saw her arrive just as he was leaving and asked the maid who the child was. When he was told, he murmured, "Puir lassie, puir lassie." He knew what trials awaited her.

The Carlyle portrait was criticized for its likeness to the picture of the artist's mother. But the similarity of pose, color and composition was wholly intentional, a deliberate variation on the same theme, and to emphasize the point Whistler called the portrait *Arrangement in Grey and Black No. 2*. Cicely Alexander's portrait is a quite different piece of music, an airy fantasy called *Harmony in Grey and Green (page 113)*. Whistler took pains with every detail, advising Mrs. Alexander on the quality of muslin in the frock her daughter was to wear in the picture, on the width of the frills on the skirt and sleeves, and even on how to have the dainty little dress laundered.

The composition is a gem of delicate but firm engineering. Cicely stands in three-quarter view, almost stiffly, holding her beribboned bonnet in her left hand. The dado on which her right hand rests, the wall behind her, and the floor all seem to be on one plane. But this apparent geometric rigidity is offset by other elements. One is Cicely's slightly pouty expression, a wonderfully human reminder that even a well-trained Victorian girl could reveal a bit of impatience. Then there are the two gossamer butterflies over Cicely's head. For all their seeming fragility they support Whistler's design with the strength of rivets. And Whistler's butterfly insignia at the left also serves a purpose, helping to direct the viewer's gaze to the top of the picture, whence it moves downward again, pauses at Cicely's aureole of pale-gold hair, falls to her hem and then to two little feet in dark-green pumps.

Years later Cicely wrote: "I'm afraid I rather considered that I was a victim all through the sittings, or standings, for he never let me change my position. I know I used to get very tired and cross, and often finished the days in tears. This was especially when he had promised to release me at a given time to go to dancing-class, but when the time came I was still standing. . . . He used to stand a good way from his canvas, and then dart at it and then dart back, and he often turned round to look in a looking-glass that hung over the mantelpiece at his back—I suppose, to see the reflection of his painting."

Cicely's assumption was correct. Like many artists, Whistler made a point of inspecting his work in a mirror because the reverse image gave him a fresh view and showed up deficiencies he might otherwise overlook. And as for his darting back and forth, other sitters confirmed this habit, recalling that Whistler so often had at his canvas with rapierlike thrusts of his long brushes that he seemed not to be painting his pictures but dueling his way through them.

As Cicely remembered it, Whistler had a softer side, too: "Although he was rather inhuman about letting me stand on for hours and hours . . . he was most kind in other ways. If a blessed black fog came up . . . . and I was allowed to get down, he never made any objection to my poking about among his paints, and I even put charcoal eyes to some of his sketches of portraits . . . and he also constantly promised to paint my doll, but this promise was never kept. . . . Of course, I was too young to appreciate Mr. Whistler himself, though afterwards we were very good friends . . . he used to come to my father's house and make at once for the portrait with his eyeglass up." Whistler had reason to scrutinize Cicely's portrait again and again. It was indisputably one of his most flawless works.

From his paintings of two elderly people and a winsome little girl, Whistler proceeded with sure hand to a portrait of a very different subject: Rosa Corder, a mistress of Whistler's rascally friend Howell. One of a harem of lady artists Howell kept, Rosa excelled at painting race horses and is said to have helped her lover produce fake masterpieces. One day Whistler glimpsed her in the street outside his studio, dressed in brown and passing a black door. He was so smitten by her proud carriage and patrician profile—and by the harmonious effect of brown on black—that he asked her to pose against a black background in the same dress and in the same regal attitude.

Rosa endured 40 sessions, standing in a doorway with a dark, shuttered room beyond. Twice she fainted from exhaustion and finally balked at any more posing. Eventually Howell himself bought the portrait. Whistler later laughingly recalled that it was "the only thing he ever paid for in his life: I was amazed when I got the check, and I only remembered some months afterwards that he paid me out of my own money which I had lent him the week before." Howell's eagerness to acquire the portrait is understandable. For Rosa, although fully dressed and standing in inky darkness, expresses a sensuality that Whistler rarely captured in his portraits.

This new note of sensuality may have reflected not only Rosa's effect on Whistler but the arrival of a new woman in his life, Maud Franklin. He and Jo Heffernan had amicably drifted apart. Even less is known about Maud's background than about Jo's. Like Jo, she had reddish hair, and she also served Whistler as model, mistress, housekeeper, cook and sometime business manager. But Maud had more polish than Jo, put on more airs. She called herself Mrs. Whistler, although she too was not invited to the homes of his starchier friends.

There is no record of how Whistler's mother reacted to the idea of another woman in residence in the Chelsea house. Possibly she was not even aware of Maud's presence, for in the mid-1870s, as her health continued to fail, she was moved to a nursing home in Hastings, a resort on the Channel coast. She remained there until her death in 1881.

Still another woman preoccupied Whistler for a time—Mrs. Frederick Leyland, wife of the Liverpool shipowner. There were rumors, probably unfounded, that Whistler's affection for her went beyond the platonic. From the portrait he made of her *(page 117)* it is obvious that he admired her warmly. For the painting, Mrs. Leyland wanted to queen it in black velvet, but Whistler overruled her. He designed a dress that had the informality of a tea gown or negligee, and posed her against filmy white-and-rose draperies that harmonized with her red hair. As in his portrait of Cicely Alexander, he created a fairy-tale princess—but one with a boudoir glow.

Whistler also painted a portrait of Mrs. Leyland's husband—spare, impressive and elegant *(page 116)*. Frederick Leyland, of all Whistler's patrons, was the most frequently mentioned in his mother's letters. He was "not only a prosperous man in Liverpool but a very cultivated gentleman of taste," and when he and his family were in residence in London "our intercourse was frequent, but Jimmy was most [often] there, dining or going with them to operas, which was healthy recreation after his long day's work."

It was Leyland who precipitated Whistler into a new phase of his career, that of interior decoration. In a letter written from Hastings in 1876, Mrs. Whistler noted that Jimmy was "decorating a spacious dining-room for Mr. Leyland" in the luxurious new London town house that Leyland had bought at 49 Prince's Gate, Hyde Park. There, Mrs. Whistler continued, her son was perched "on ladders and scaffoldings using his palette and studio brushes! No wonder he looks thin."

Whatever the cost in energy, Whistler had the exhilarating sense that he was creating a masterpiece. The project in which he was taking part was the talk of artistic London. Leyland, whose own mother had sold pies on the streets of Liverpool, seemed intent on proving to the world that he had come a long way from his humble beginnings; he proposed to make his new house as impressive as a Venetian palace. The

Whistler made these preliminary sketches for panels he planned to paint in the dining room of his patron Frederick Leyland. Opposite are his designs for three tall window shutters; below is his satirical sketch for a panel showing himself as a poor peacock scrapping with a furious rich peacock, Leyland. A photograph of the actual Peacock Room, bought and brought to the United States by one of Whistler's American patrons, appears on pages 118 and 119.

outside was to remain untouched, so that it would not obtrude in the dress parade of uniform mansions facing Hyde Park. The interior, however, was to be wholly transformed. Structural alterations were being handled by a noted architect, Norman Shaw, while decorations were being supervised by a younger architect, Henry Jeckyll, who hoped thereby to make his reputation. A number of other experts on design were also consulted, including William Morris and the painter Edward Burne-Jones, a disciple of Rossetti and follower of the Pre-Raphaelite style. For the old Pre-Raphaelite Brothers, in fact, the Leyland town-house project was a particularly happy event. They were to be abundantly represented by their own works; Leyland owned nine paintings by Rossetti and one by Millais.

Whistler was invited to paint a dado in the entrance hall, to which a magnificent staircase and a balustrade of gilt bronze had been transplanted from an old Tudor mansion that was being demolished. The design he decided on for the dado was "delicate sprigs of pale rose and white flowers in the Japanese taste." But this assignment was to prove only a warm-up for his main show.

At Rossetti's urging, Leyland had bought Whistler's *La Princesse du Pays de la Porcelaine,* the portrait of young Christine Spartali that her father had rejected. The plan was to hang it in the dining room over a mantel. The decoration of the room itself was supervised by Henry Jeckyll. He had had the walls covered with £1,000 worth of antique-yellow leather adorned with reddish flowers and pomegranates —the insignia of Catherine of Aragon, Henry VIII's first wife, who had brought the leather from Spain. Jeckyll had also created an ornate ceil-

ing studded with glass gas fixtures that looked like Japanese lanterns and had lined the room with carved shelves to hold Leyland's collection of blue-and-white porcelain.

When Whistler saw where his *Princesse* was to reign he protested to Leyland that the red flowers and the red border on the rug would clash with her brown-and-yellow color scheme. He proposed to tone down the flowers and cut the border off the rug. Leyland assented and went off to Liverpool, innocently leaving Whistler in charge. Then Whistler found that daubing at the flowers only made the clash of colors worse. With typical impetuosity he decided to abandon halfway measures and cover the antique-yellow leather walls entirely in blue paint and embellish this with giant gold peacocks. He had been exposed to real, shrieking peacocks in Rossetti's back yard and had already made peacock sketches for a project that had fallen through.

Before long Whistler was in a peacock frenzy. He recruited two Chelsea neighbors, Walter and Harry Greaves, the artistically inclined boatmen who often rowed Whistler on the Thames on sketching forays. Each morning at seven they joined Whistler in the Leyland dining room, clambered up ladders, spilled gold and blue paint in their hair, and toiled day after week after month. As the project went on, Whistler grew almost hysterically euphoric. He grandly invited people to drop in and watch him at work on "the loveliest thing in the world." He shouted greetings from his scaffold, hopped down to serve tea among the paintpots and swept one of his lady callers into a waltz. Queen Victoria's daughter, Princess Louise, paid him a visit, and so did Lord Redesdale, and the Duchess of . . . well, according to the artist, just "everybody." Whistler had staged a Victorian happening.

The press got wind of it and sent reporters. To make their jobs easier the painter issued printed leaflets explaining his peacocks. When accounts of the work in progress appeared in the press, casual strollers dropped in to see for themselves. Among them one day was Jeckyll, wondering what terrible fate had overtaken Catherine of Aragon's leather and the other features he had so lovingly planned for the room. He was stunned. Whistler had taken to painting peacock eyes on the ceiling, gold paint was spattered on the floor, the air seemed to be raining gold. None too stable a personality at best, young Jeckyll cowered among the throng of sightseers, then left the Leyland house in a state of shock. Back home in his bedroom he got down on his knees and began painting his own floor gold. He went completely mad and a few weeks later died in an asylum. Whistler's comment when he heard of it was matter-of-fact: "To be sure, that is the effect I always have on people."

Inevitably, Leyland showed up from Liverpool to see what in heaven was going on. Far from approving, he accused Whistler of ruining the whole decorative scheme for the room. Most of all he resented having his home turned into a show place for Whistler's antics. To end the affair he asked the artist how much he owed him. Whistler said 2,000 guineas. Leyland thought the fee exorbitant and, after seeking Rossetti's advice, paid £1,000. Whistler was infuriated, not so much at the reduced sum but at being paid in pounds. The difference between a

---

TWO-DAY BUCKWHEAT PANCAKES

½ package active dry yeast
OR
½ cake compressed yeast
*½ cup lukewarm water (used in two
   ¼-cup portions)*
2 cups scalded milk
2 cups buckwheat flour
½ teaspoon salt
1 tablespoon molasses
1 teaspoon baking soda

Dissolve ½ package OR ½ cake yeast in ¼ cup lukewarm water. Scald 2 cups milk and cool to lukewarm. To the cooled milk add the yeast mixture, 2 cups buckwheat flour, ½ teaspoon salt, and beat hard for a couple of minutes. Cover and let stand at room temperature overnight.

Next morning, mix in 1 tablespoon molasses, 1 teaspoon baking soda and another ¼ cup lukewarm water.

As a child in New England, Whistler developed a taste for buckwheat cakes that he continued to indulge at the large breakfasts he gave in London. He is believed to have used the recipe above.

"UNCLE JIM'S BOOK OF PANCAKES," THE FILTER PRESS, 1967

guinea (21 shillings) and a pound (20 shillings) was trifling. But only tradesmen were paid in pounds; guineas were a status symbol of almost mystical import.

Leyland returned to Liverpool with the expectation that Whistler would pack up and get out. But Whistler had vengeance in mind. He stayed on and decorated one end of the dining room—the end Leyland would face when seated at the head of his table—with splashy allegorical caricatures of a poor peacock (himself) and a rich peacock (Leyland). Under the rich bird's talons he painted the pile of extra shillings he felt he should have received.

One can only imagine what further vitriolic caprices Whistler might have painted had not Mrs. Leyland arrived unexpectedly in London. Letting herself into her house, she overheard Whistler remark about her husband: "Well, you know, what can you expect from a parvenu?" She ordered him to leave at once, and when he returned a few days later he was refused admittance.

Although Whistler's golden birds fatally overpowered the display of Leyland's delicate blue-and-white porcelains, they were a triumph in their own right, proof that Whistler's flair for interior design was genuine. And they made a dashing setting for formal dinner parties. They may have struck some viewers, however, as birds of ill omen, with something faintly insane in their flamboyance, as if they were the fantasies of a man fighting compulsively to assert and defend himself.

Leyland might easily have had the insulting rich peacock painted over or concealed by another picture. But he stoutheartedly kept it on view, along with Whistler's appealing *Princesse* on the opposite wall. The entire room *(pages 118-119)* could hardly be surpassed as a lively conversation starter for his dinner guests.

Determined that the infamy of the peacock affair be remembered, Whistler later painted three more cruel caricatures of Leyland—one of them again showing him as an avaricious bird—and sold them. Today they serve less as reminders of what Whistler regarded as Leyland's penuriousness than of the painful truth that Whistler had behaved like an idiot.

By the time of the Peacock Room episode he was already known in artistic circles as a man of notable verve and independence of mind. But the scandal of the Leyland affair entrenched him in the public eye as a brilliant eccentric, a role he played with increasing alacrity. He took to making a ritual of Sunday breakfasts in his studio for 10 to 20 guests—royalty, social lions, patrons, painters, poets and journalists. People were invited for noon, although they might be kept waiting two hours, with Whistler nowhere to be seen, only heard splashing in his bathtub. But when he appeared, natty in his white duck suit, fizzing with high spirits and funny stories, everybody forgave him. Buckwheat cakes were the specialty of the house and, whenever obtainable, corn. Whistler himself hardly ever sat down or ate anything. Instead he orbited the table telling jokes and pouring wine, synchronizing his words and movements like a trained actor, building up suspense by poising the bottle over a goblet, pouring at the precise instant when a

Although Whistler never sat for Walter Greaves, his Chelsea neighbor and sometime pupil, he appeared in a number of Greaves' sketches, including *Whistler Rowing on the Thames (right)*. Chelsea boatmen by profession, Walter and his brother, Harry, fell in with Whistler in the late 1850s; for a number of years they hovered about him, learning how to draw and paint while performing such tasks as rowing Whistler up and down the Thames as the artist etched his "Thames Set."

pause was most dramatic. The food was not always copious. One guest, who came especially to see the host's pictures, rebelled: "No, Whistler, I have paid three shillings and sixpence for a cab to come here and I have eaten one egg, and I will look at no pictures!"

Whistler's dinners were equally spirited. Since his house was sparsely furnished, guests perched gamely on packing boxes or crates. On the day of one party he decided to redo the dining-room walls in pale yellow with a suggestion of pink; the guests that night took home little souvenirs of pinkish-yellow paint on their clothes. Although Whistler provided such elegant touches as exotic flower arrangements and pottery displays, dining at his house was often a genteel version of "roughing it," and fashionable folk loved it for being so very amusingly bohemian.

To other people's dinners Whistler often came an hour late but was invariably the life of the party. He and Mark Twain are said to have met for the first time at a dinner at which each of them asked the hostess who that noisy fellow was. Later Twain came to dine at Whistler's, and on the tram he took to get there he made up a jingle about the busy conductors with their ticket punches: "Punch, brothers. punch with care; punch in the presence of the passenjaire." Whistler shared Twain's love of jingles, his favorite being the most famous question in the annals of zoology: "How much wood would a woodchuck chuck, if a woodchuck could chuck wood?" Incorrigibly playful, Whistler had a stunt of imitating two angry men shouting at one another; he liked to put on this performance outside people's doors. And when they ran out to investigate the row, all they found was Whistler, laughing at them.

He seemed always to be on stage. Before entering a room full of people he would visibly preen, ruffling up his curls and smoothing his clothes. Then, as if from the wings, would come the grand entrance of little Mr. Whistler, dressed as only Mr. Whistler dressed. He considered himself a living canvas, to be covered with patches of white (his duck suits), off-whites (his straw hats), and accents of black (his patent-leather pumps and the ribbons that fluttered from his hat or around his neck). He enjoyed accenting himself with other tones as well. Once, en route to a dinner party, he ran into an artist friend, Val Prinsep, who noted that Whistler had thrust a large, salmon-colored silk handkerchief into the top of his black waistcoat, just below an expanse of white shirt. Fearing that the handkerchief might slip out, Prinsep tucked it deeper into Whistler's waistcoat. "Good God!" roared Whistler. "What are you doing? You've destroyed my precious note of color." He pulled the handkerchief back into sight and went on his way, waving the white cane he affected.

Whistler also made much of a lock of white hair that sprouted suddenly over his forehead and stood out like a little plume among his black curls. It came, he once explained, from a head wound incurred on his military adventure to South America. He wore it proudly, like Cyrano's panache, teasing it into prominence and always pushing back his hat brim so that the white dash could be properly admired.

Despite these vanities Whistler gave not the slightest impression of being effeminate. Many of his friends, and even his enemies, remarked on this anomaly. He was simply a supreme individualist, with a zest for life and a willingness to share it. The door at his house was almost always open. Models, fellow artists, students, friends, strangers swarmed in. Often there was music in the air; Whistler hired a hurdy-gurdy player to perform in the back yard, and permitted a parasitic young pianist to live with him for more than a year. "Who else is there," he asked, "to whom we could say, 'Play,' and he would play?" Irate bill collectors were also frequently on the premises. One night an angry art dealer came to collect some money owed him. He was told that Whistler was out, but he heard the master's voice in the studio. He rushed in and found Whistler painting while Walter Greaves held a candle to provide light. Whistler was undismayed at the intrusion. "You are the very man I want," he cried, "hold a candle!" Pressed into service, the dealer waited until the sketch was done, whereupon Whistler grabbed it and dashed into the night, leaving his creditor still holding the candle.

At times Whistler's house appeared to be Puck's enchanted forest, a light-hearted haven of pranks. But behind the façade of foolishness there was an artist earnestly at work. Whistler was embarked on a series of paintings that were ultimately to secure his place in the pantheon of modern art: his Nocturnes, largely inspired by night scenes along the Thames near Chelsea.

As indicated in the titles he gave these works—*Nocturne in Blue and Silver, Nocturne in Black and Gold*—Whistler was still concerned with color, this time with the more muted chromatics of the darkness. But he was in addition concerned with something else—depicting the sense of space, of void, that the nighttime generates. In such a setting people and objects are discerned only dimly; precise outlines disappear. And so Whistler ruthlessly dissolved forms and substituted the implicit for the explicit, requiring the viewer to apply his own imagination to what he saw. The Nocturnes were distillations, not so much of scenes as of moods.

In search of material, Whistler customarily recruited the Greaves brothers to row him on the river at night. In a friendly exchange of skills he taught them to use the brush and they taught him to use the oar with a special stroke called the Waterman's Jerk. Some decades earlier their father had piloted the great J. M. W. Turner, another Chelsea luminary, on similar excursions. But whereas Turner's passion was for sunsets, Whistler preferred the hours that followed, painting from nightfall to dawn. Between them, it seems, the two artists got the sun down and the dark installed.

On his rowboat cruises Whistler seldom attempted to paint; rather, he scribbled notes, sketched on scraps of paper and stored up impressions. After an experience had marinated a bit in his head, he would get to work in his studio, confirming in paint William Wordsworth's observation about his own field of endeavor: "poetry . . . takes its origins from emotion recollected in tranquillity."

Years later Walter Greaves recalled how carefully Whistler had worked on the Nocturnes, particularly their backgrounds. Often he chose to paint on wood rather than on canvas, selecting, perhaps, a panel of mahogany to insure a dark ground close to the basic tone he wanted. Then on his palette he would arrange large quantities of dry pigments of different tones and moisten them with a mixture of sticky resins and turpentine; he used it in such abundance that he called it his "sauce." At the start the panel was usually propped on his easel, but as he washed different tones across it, it had to be laid on the floor to keep the sauce from running off. At a cursory glance his backgrounds might appear to be of one tone; actually they contain many shades and nuances of color that impart the shimmering look he sought.

The hints of boats, shorelines, lanterns and bridges in his Nocturnes testify to one of Whistler's most extraordinary skills. He was able to create an object or person with what looked like a mere flick of paint, often packing more life into these "swipes" than other artists could achieve by plodding effort. He owed this gift in part to the Oriental influence he had amalgamated into his style; the swift swipes were reminiscent of the sure, clean strokes of a Japanese calligrapher. Ironically, this instant life-giving touch laid Whistler open to charges of carelessness, but in fact the technique had taken him years to perfect.

The Nocturnes were not all scenes of the river; some were views of the popular local amusement park, Cremorne Gardens, with its flickering lanterns, fireworks and dim revelers. Another was a view of an empty street, *Nocturne in Grey and Gold: Chelsea Snow*, in which a solitary figure moves toward a glowing window. Lest anybody wax sentimental about this frozen traveler in the night, Whistler hastened to explain: "I care nothing for the past, present or future of the black figure, placed there because the black was wanted at that spot. All that I know is that my combination of grey and gold is the basis of the picture. Now this is precisely what my friends cannot grasp."

The Nocturnes had no wide popularity in Whistler's time, although their ambience of muted mystery, of peace mingled with loneliness, appealed strongly to certain sensitive temperaments. Such poets as William Ernest Henley and Arthur Symons, as well as the composer Claude Debussy and the painter Georges Seurat, were especially attuned to these moody little masterpieces. Whistler himself certainly took pride and comfort in them. They were uniquely his own creations, carrying his own trademark, speaking a visual language he had invented. Moreover, the Nocturnes led into a private realm where he had no need to outwit his adversaries, where he was no longer an actor capering for an audience. In these works identities were lost, time and place had little meaning, nothing mattered except the transitory beauty he had evoked.

The Nocturnes were nonetheless destined to bring great unhappiness into Whistler's life. In May 1877 the new Grosvenor Gallery opened in London. A private exhibition hall built by the banker Sir Coutts Lindsay, it was located near Grosvenor Square, convenient for the carriages of Mayfair, and its main room, decorated in crimson damask and green velvet, had a Medici grandeur. The building included a restaurant, where a gala opening banquet attended by the Prince of Wales was the sensation of the social season.

Among those invited to exhibit at the new gallery were Whistler, Rossetti, Hunt, Millais and Burne-Jones. Whistler was represented by a couple of portraits and several Nocturnes, one of which was *Nocturne in Black and Gold: The Falling Rocket (page 134)*, a study of a night fireworks display exploding over Cremorne Gardens, a spectacle Whistler always loved to watch. All of his entries made a poor impression; their subdued colors and simple patterns were wholly eclipsed by the ornate décor of the gallery. Millais, scrutinizing one Whistler painting, observed righteously, "It's damned clever, it's a damned sight *too* clever"—as if there had to be something tricky in such low-key simplicity.

A far crueler comment came from John Ruskin, whose ardor for spiritual uplift in art made him singularly hostile to the very different ardors of Whistler. Ruskin reviewed the entire exhibition, which he generally disliked, in his own magazine, *Fors Clavigera*—literally translated, "Fortune bearing a club." The club that fortune swung at Whistler had a powerful impact, for Ruskin—now the unchallenged arbiter of English tastes in art—picked out *The Falling Rocket* and its price tag (200 guineas) for special abuse: "For Mr. Whistler's sake, no less than for the protection of the purchaser [the Grosvenor] ought not to have admitted works into the gallery in which the ill-educated conceit of the artist so nearly approached the aspect of wilful imposture. I have seen and heard much of cockney impudence before now, but never expected to hear a coxcomb ask two hundred guineas for flinging a pot of paint in the public's face."

Not only was the insult totally undeserved, but it was peculiarly painful for a man of Whistler's sensibilities to withstand. For the rest of his life almost everything he said or did was to some degree an act of retaliation—and his first retaliatory act was to sue Ruskin for libel.

Portraits and Peacocks

By the late 1860s Whistler had absorbed a variety of painting experiences and returned to a field familiar to him, portraiture. While it was based on reality, he felt that it was open to much pictorial invention. He had two essential goals: to evoke a sense of personality and convey an impression that a private moment in the life of the sitter had been preserved and to demonstrate that a portrait is not just a more or less authentic likeness but also a study in color and arrangement.

In the delicate portrait at right, for example, Whistler leaves us in no doubt as to how young Miss Alexander looked, but he devotes equal care to the overall effect of the picture. The background, flat and muted in color, has a linear, almost Japanese quality; the floor is depicted in rhythmic patterns that create a confection of soft color and texture resembling nothing so much as sea foam. Whistler's butterfly insignia at left and the sprays of daisies barely nodding into view at right are no mere accidental touches, but deliberate accents intended both to complement the girl's charms and the painting's general design.

To achieve his goals Whistler drove himself and his models ruthlessly. Repeated rubbings-out and new starts marked his agonizing attempts at perfection. Out of scores of portraits that he began, only about a dozen were completed to his satisfaction, but they bear witness to his unique blend of reality and imagination.

The air of fragile innocence that Whistler produced in this portrait of Cicely Alexander is all the more remarkable because he compelled the child—only nine when she posed—to endure some 70 sessions, often hours long. She bore it all more or less patiently but years later confessed: "I'm still afraid all my memories only show that I was a very grumbling disagreeable little girl."

Harmony in Grey and Green:
Miss Cicely Alexander, c. 1872-1874

Arrangement in Grey and Black No. 1: The Artist's Mother, exhibited 1872

Like many popular and widely reproduced masterpieces, Whistler's portrait of his mother has become almost invisible, an image by now so familiar that it is seldom carefully scrutinized. Yet there is much to see in the painting. The likeness of this fine-boned, small-featured little lady is precisely and beautifully rendered; the artist once said, in response to a compliment on the excellence of the face and figure, "Yes, one does like to make one's mummy just as nice as possible." But, as the title of the work indicates, Whistler intended to focus attention not just on his mother but on his overall arrangement of forms and colors. To offset the figure, he structured a careful linear pattern-by way of the wall against which she is silhouetted, the fall of drapery at the left and the stark rectangles of the black picture frames—Whistler's own etchings, including *(at left) Black Lion Wharf (pages 156-157)*.

He adopted a similar approach in his portrait of the writer Thomas Carlyle *(right)*, using picture frames and the bold line of a baseboard to organize the background for the profile figure. But he also accomplished his other goal, the revelation of character, in the care he paid to specific details about his illustrious sitter. Carlyle's gloved right hand resting on his walking stick, the cock of his head, the slouch of his body, illuminate this brilliant description of a wise but weary man.

Arrangement in Grey and Black No. 2: Thomas Carlyle, 1872-1873

Whistler's problem in painting this portrait of the industrialist Frederick Leyland was self-imposed: he set out to depict a full-length figure dressed in black against a black background. The pitfalls were large. Black on black could lead to a total loss of definition of the figure, and by showing it from head to foot Whistler risked the danger of ending up with a flattened image like that on a playing card. But he was a gambler, and his gamble paid off, despite an added complication he had not foreseen. Leyland was a busy man with little time to spare. Beset by the difficulty of painting Leyland's stance convincingly, Whistler hired a stand-in, whom he posed in the nude.

Whistler had less trouble with Mrs. Leyland *(opposite)*, even though she originally wanted to be shown in black like her husband. Particularly delighted with her red hair—two of his mistresses had been so endowed—Whistler persuaded her that she could best set off this natural asset by posing in a dress of soft hues. The result was a delicate yet rich color scheme. Although the portrait was left unfinished—the hands and other details are very sketchily painted—Whistler succeeded in memorializing Mrs. Leyland as a gentle vision of elegance.

In addition to these portraits, Leyland also bought Whistler's *La Princesse du Pays de la Porcelaine* and installed it in his new London mansion over the mantel in the dining room. Lined with shelves to hold his collection of blue-and-white porcelain, the room *(overleaf)* had been decorated by a leading architect. Leyland had every reason to expect that Whistler would be delighted by the honor accorded his lovely Oriental fantasy, but he was soon to be disabused of this notion.

Arrangement in Black: Portrait of F. R. Leyland, 1873

116

Mrs. Frederick R. Leyland, 1873

Although pleased that his *Princesse (at right, above the fireplace)* had been chosen to keynote Leyland's porcelain, Whistler was deeply upset by the room's color scheme, which he claimed clashed with the painting. Leyland gave the artist permission to make alterations. But Whistler fell into a frenzy of creation and slathered blue paint over the leather on the walls, gilded the ceiling and emblazoned three shutters with peacocks. He also "signed" the room in four places with his butterfly, once at the top right corner of the central shutter *(far right)*.

When Leyland saw what Whistler had done he was shocked. They quarreled over how much Whistler should be paid for his work, and the artist, embittered at the settlement, decided to take revenge. He returned to the house and, opposite his *Princesse*, painted a new panel *(above)*. In it he showed a rich peacock covered with gold coins (Leyland) scrapping with a poor peacock (Whistler); under the claws of the rich bird is a pile of silver coins —the money Whistler felt he was owed.

The fate of the Peacock Room proved happier than the relationship between artist and patron. In 1904 the American Charles Freer bought the paneled room from a London dealer and in 1919 presented it to the American people. It is now in the Freer Gallery of Art in Washington, D.C.

Harmony in Blue and Gold: The Peacock Room, 1876-1877

119

VI

A Scandalous Trial

"It is the most debased style of criticism I have had thrown at me yet," said Whistler, as he read Ruskin's diatribe on *The Falling Rocket.* At the time, he was alone with an artist friend, George Boughton, in the smoking room of the Arts Club, one of several to which he belonged in London. Hesitantly, Boughton had shown him a copy of Ruskin's magazine, *Fors Clavigera,* with its scurrilous charge that Whistler had flung "a pot of paint in the public's face," and that his price of 200 guineas for the painting *(page 134)* was exorbitant to boot. For once, Whistler was unable to mask dismay with a quip.

"Sounds rather like libel," ventured Boughton.

"Well, that I shall try to find out," said Whistler, lighting a cigarette and leaving at once to look into the possibilities of legal action.

In afteryears Lady Burne-Jones, wife of the artist, recalled that when Ruskin heard of the upstart Whistler's plan to go to court to challenge him, he gloated that the prospect of a trial was "nuts and nectar." This response suggests an overwrought state of mind, which was indeed the case. Ruskin had long been in emotional turmoil. His marriage to Euphemia Gray had been annulled on the ground that the union had never been consummated, and Euphemia had subsequently married Ruskin's protégé, the painter John Millais. Ruskin's next encounter with love was equally disastrous. At 39 he was seriously smitten with 10-year-old Rose La Touche, daughter of a wealthy Irish banker who had hired him to give his children drawing lessons. When Rose was 18, he astounded her by proposing. She asked for three years to make up her mind and eventually turned him down via Charles Augustus Howell, Ruskin's occasional secretary, whom he had sent to plead his cause. In 1875 Rose died and Ruskin was devastated, suffering a brief mental breakdown.

Added to his personal torments, Ruskin had long been consumed by a messianic conviction that art should serve a moral purpose. He had exhausted himself by a torrential outpouring of books on architecture and art, including the five-volume *Modern Painters*, as well as tracts on geology, biology and social welfare and a volume called *Notes on*

Staring shrewdly and a bit belligerently out of his own portrait, Whistler regards the world with a cool detachment. During the decade after he painted this self-image, he achieved some of his greatest works, and met the cruelest test his battered reputation would ever face: a trial in which he was forced to defend his artistic style and its worth —the most humiliating and difficult challenge any artist could accept.

Arrangement in Grey: Self-Portrait, 1871-1873

The trim, compact White House in Chelsea where Whistler lived and worked was designed by the architect E. W. Godwin. In addition to dictating the unusually clean lines of the house, totally at variance with the fussy, gabled style popular in Victorian London, Whistler fashioned an artistic "arrangement" reminiscent of his paintings out of the house's colors: the white bricks were counterpointed by a green slate roof and a bright blue door.

the Construction of Sheepfolds, a plea for Christian unity that had a fair sale among Cumberland farmers who took its title literally. He was also the first to fill the prestigious new Slade Professorship of Fine Art at Oxford, and was a frequent lecturer to other audiences.

Eloquence was Ruskin's great gift. By making art sound as exhilarating as victory in battle or conversion to true faith, he roused masses of people to an awareness of beauty. As for his judgments, by today's standards they run from the remarkably perceptive to the plainly preposterous. Rightly, he extolled Gothic architecture. He discerned the greatness of Turner and the virtues of the Pre-Raphaelites. Yet, while eulogizing such minor painters as Clarkson Stanfield, who produced a number of tepid seascapes, and Kate Greenaway, who specialized in sentimental portraits of children, he slapped down Rembrandt. In the shifting currents of taste, Ruskin stands as a salutary reminder that today's treasure may readily become tomorrow's trash—and that trash may turn to treasure.

Ruskin's hostility to Whistler was not a sudden development. Four years before his blast at *The Falling Rocket* he had used his Oxford podium to denounce Whistler's art as "absolute rubbish." If only for their clashing views on the need for moral uplift in art, Ruskin and Whistler were natural enemies. But there were probably other causes. Ruskin must have resented Whistler's close friendship with Howell, the repository of many indiscreet Ruskin confidences about his difficulties in love and his sometimes disorganized personal finances. Moreover, it is likely that Whistler's lack of homage offended Ruskin, who took a schoolmasterish pleasure in bestowing his affections, his scoldings and his generosity upon young artists. However it was compounded, Ruskin's animosity made him a formidable foe.

The case of Whistler versus Ruskin was destined to be history's most celebrated trial on an art issue. Whistler was suing for £1,000 in damages, and the trial was scheduled to begin 16 months after the alleged libel was published in the July 1877 issue of *Fors Clavigera*. The interim was for Whistler a time of anxiety and acute financial worry. By insinuating that his work was not only sloppy but overpriced, Ruskin had effectively curtailed Whistler's income. People became loath to admit that they owned Whistlers, and even young Cicely Alexander was suddenly ashamed of her lovely portrait. Whistler was used to being short of cash, but now the pinch was drastic; when he took a cab he often had to direct the driver to a friend's house to borrow the fare. To ease the financial crisis, he resolved to take students in his own studio. And, lacking room for a proper atelier, he decided he must build a new and larger home.

Whistler picked the worst possible time for so extravagant a project, yet its very recklessness cheered him. He recruited his friend, the brilliant and controversial architect Edward Godwin, with whom he had many ideas in common about art and decoration, and together they conceived a compact three-story residence with a studio on the top floor and space for the proposed school on the second. It was built on Tite Street in Chelsea with a view of the Thames.

Surprisingly modern in its clean lines, white brick walls and green slate roof, the White House, as it came to be called, was an architectural rebuke to all the fussy Queen Anne gables and Gothic portals of the day. As a result, the Metropolitan Board of Works, which passed on the suitability of all new buildings in London, required Godwin to add a few moldings, window frames and redeeming doodads. However new its look, the house did not escape the age-old vicissitudes of building; it took longer to erect than planned, was altered during construction and cost more than estimated.

To meet expenses, Whistler had to pawn, sell or mortgage everything he could lay hands on. Howell gave him £10 and a sealskin coat for a portrait of the actor Henry Irving *(page 136)* and helped him more substantially by persuading the publisher Henry Graves to issue engravings of *Carlyle* and several other works. Graves also offered Whistler £1,000—engraving rights included—to produce a portrait of Benjamin Disraeli. But all Whistler got was the humiliation of having the great "Dizzy" turn him down. The Prime Minister chose instead to pose for Millais.

Whistler also sought to augment his income through his always-popular etchings—both reprints and new prints. In the period leading up to the libel trial, he endured, as he put it, a "fiendish slavery to the press." Toiling long hours over hand presses, he turned out a series of London street scenes for such magazines as *Vanity Fair* and *Piccadilly*. In the process he became fascinated by the century-old technique of lithography, which he learned from the noted printer Thomas Way. Almost overnight Whistler became proficient at drawing with greased chalks on lithographer's stones and pulling prints of exquisite delicacy. In this medium as in others his extreme artistic sensibilities were backed by a firm-handed craftsmanship. Slight as he was, Whistler's muscular arms and shoulders enabled him to handle the various tools of his profession with superb control, and to create impalpable effects with masterly precision. He was a magician at turning the ephemeral into the permanent.

During this period of odd jobs and rush assignments, Whistler also produced 19 small drawings to illustrate the catalogue of a private collection of blue-and-white Nankin pottery, all in a direct, detailed style that befitted such a factual compilation. The butterfly, it seemed, could turn into a laboring beetle when necessary.

Across the street from Thomas Way's printing establishment was the Gaiety Theater. Whistler not only produced a lithograph called *The Gaiety Stage Door*, but made friends with the troupe of actors inside. Enchanted by him, they put on a fly-by-night farce, *The Grasshopper*, in which the artist himself was caricatured, and a Whistleresque painting, used as a comic prop, was shown to look equally well upside down or right side up. Far from offended, Whistler laughed along with the rest of the audience.

He increasingly invited caricature, for his upcurling mustache and brows, his impish strut and cocky white forelock were catnip to cartoonists. Now, with his growing notoriety, he became the subject of an increasing number of spoofs and take-offs. He appeared in *Punch*, drawn by his old friend George du Maurier, and was lampooned in other periodicals by the popular London caricaturists known as "Spy" and "Ape." He gave the impression of sharing their fun and striking comic poses to make their jobs easier. At times, one suspects, he was his own burlesque of himself.

Resolved to appear unperturbed by his critical drubbing, Whistler in 1878 sent several works to the second Grosvenor Gallery show, including a few Nocturnes and *Arrangement in Black and White No. 1: The Young American*, a portrait of his mistress Maud Franklin, looking a bit brassy with her hand on her hip *(page 100)*. Although Maud was English, the picture suggested some of the freshness, the mixture of innocence and crudity that Henry James was putting into such fictional heroines as Isabel Archer, in *The Portrait of a Lady*, and Daisy Miller, whose sad tale was published the same year. Whistler never explained the title of *The Young American*; most likely he simply saw certain American traits in Maud.

As it happened, Henry James himself visited the second Grosvenor exhibit and reviewed it for the American weekly *The Nation*. Although he and Whistler were to become the two most illustrious American expatriates in England, they never became close friends. James, nine years younger than Whistler, aspired to fit decorously into British high society, and succeeded. Whistler preferred to dazzle his way wherever he went, decorum be hanged. As a critic, James reacted favorably to the Grosvenor show, rating it considerably higher than the Royal Academy exhibition of the same year. But, saving his praise for the entries of Burne-Jones and George Boughton, he was only mildly impressed by Whistler's latest paintings: "Mr. Whistler's productions are pleasant things to have about, so long as one regards them as simple objects

—as incidents of furniture or decoration. The spectator's quarrel with them begins when he feels it to be expected of him to regard them as pictures. His manner is very much that of the French 'Impressionists'." In Paris in 1876, at a show of the Impressionists' work, James had seen paintings by Monet, Pissarro, Sisley and Renoir. It was a case of instant dislike. "None . . . show signs of possessing first-rate talent," he wrote, and trounced the artists further because they "abjure virtue altogether . . . send detail to the dogs and concentrate themselves on general expression." Many years later James warmed up appreciably to both the Impressionists and Whistler.

As for the critics, their treatment of Whistler at the second Grosvenor showing did not stop at condescension but moved to shabby insult. His new Nocturnes—more studies of Chelsea—were dismissed as "a diet of fog," and *The Young American* inspired one reviewer to observe: "Mr. Whistler is in great force. Last year some of his life-size portraits were without feet; here we have a curiously shaped young lady ostentatiously showing her foot, which is a pretty large one."

By now, Whistler had become a favorite whipping boy, always good for laughs. People began to look forward to the libel trial; they expected it to be a barrel of fun—and they were proved right.

The trial took place on November 25 and 26, 1878, in the Court of Exchequer Division, His Lordship Sir John Walter Huddleston presiding. Ruskin was not present. He had had another mental breakdown and had been delirious for days. By now he had recovered, but his doctor personally assured Judge Huddleston that the strain of the trial would be injurious to his patient.

In his absence, Ruskin had appointed the popular painter Burne-Jones to support his case, assisted by the equally popular William Frith and Tom Taylor, art critic of *The Times* and editor of *Punch*. Whistler had counted on a rescue squad of various London artists to defend him in the witness box, but one by one they had backed out. In the end his major witnesses were William Rossetti, who was not enthusiastic about *The Falling Rocket*, the picture that had aroused Ruskin's ire, but felt that Whistler had set a fair price for it, and Albert Moore, who had no reservations whatever about his friend's work.

Serjeant Parry, one of the plaintiff's counsel, opened with a capsule history of Whistler's career, then turned to examine his client. During this questioning Whistler inexplicably stated that he had been born in St. Petersburg, Russia. On cross-examination by Ruskin's counsel, Sir John Holker, Whistler managed to establish in the record that his works had been exhibited at the Royal Academy and that his etchings were included in collections at the British Museum and Windsor Castle. He added that since Ruskin's attack, his Nocturnes no longer commanded decent prices.

Whistler was asked to define a Nocturne ("an arrangement of line, form and color," he put it) and to explain *The Falling Rocket*. "It is a night piece," he said, "and represents the fireworks at Cremorne."

"Not a view of Cremorne?" asked Sir John Holker.

"If it were called a view of Cremorne, it would certainly bring about nothing but disappointment on the part of the beholders. [Laughter.] It is an artistic arrangement."

Hearing a picture described as merely "an artistic arrangement" would not now surprise anyone reasonably familiar with modern art. But in Victorian times this was a revolutionary—a downright subversive—concept. Most Victorians devoutly believed that nature should be depicted with microscopic accuracy. How could they grasp a Whistler Nocturne in which reality was blurred almost beyond recognition or wholly ignored?

To orthodox art lovers the loss of detail and the simplification of form in Whistler's work meant a loss of credibility. To Whistler the eliminations were a means of strengthening the abstract power of his art. To his detractors the dominance of a single color like blue was a distortion of the truth. To Whistler limiting the range of color produced an intensification of poetic mood.

These matters—although relevant today—held no import for the cross-examiner. Sir John moved to other ground. Whistler agreed that 200 guineas was "a pretty good price for a picture." Then Ruskin's counsel pressed the point: "It is what we who are not artists should call a stiffish price?"

"I think it very likely it would be so." *(Laughter.)*

After obtaining an admission from Whistler that his pictures reflected "some eccentricities," Sir John wanted to know how long it took him to "knock off" a Nocturne. "Oh," said Whistler, "I knock off one possibly in a couple of days [Laughter.]—one day to do the work, and another to finish it."

"And that was the labor for which you asked two hundred guineas?" Sir John asked.

"No, it was for the knowledge gained through a lifetime."

This clever comeback received warm applause from the spectators —not that they were much in sympathy with Whistler, but like an audience at a play, they relished a brisk bit of dialogue. His Lordship Judge Huddleston warned that he would clear the court if there were any more such outbursts.

One of the Nocturnes that had been exhibited at the first Grosvenor exhibit—*Nocturne in Blue and Gold: Old Battersea Bridge (page 135)*—was produced, and Judge Huddleston got into the act, asking Whistler, "Is this part of the picture at the top Old Battersea Bridge?"

"Your Lordship is too close at present to the picture to perceive the effect which I intended to produce at a distance. The spectator is supposed to be looking down the river towards London."

Then His Lordship, all unknowingly, asked the most important question to be raised throughout the trial: "Are those figures on the top of the bridge intended for people?"

"They are just what you like," Whistler replied.

Well aware of the vital nature of this terse exchange, Whistler years later expanded on it in a compendium of critical comments that had been made about his art. In this volume he also incorporated what he considered to be his most devastating ripostes. Not only did he rewrite his answer to the judge, but the question as well. He had been asked, Whistler reported, "Do you say that this is a correct representation of Battersea Bridge?" He reported that his reply was: "I did not intend it to be a 'correct' portrait of the bridge. . . . As to what the picture represents, that depends upon who looks at it."

The whole story of modern art lies in that last sentence. What neither the trial judge nor Ruskin understood was that a fundamental new esthetic was emerging, in which the true beauty of a work of art lay in the experience of the painter of the work and of the individual who viewed it, rather than in any object represented on the canvas. According to this esthetic the object represented was no longer as important as the interpretation the artist chose to make of it—and that was precisely what Whistler was about. As for the painting of Battersea Bridge, he went on to explain at the trial, "My whole scheme was only to bring about a certain harmony of color."

Unaware that art history had been made, the court adjourned at this point and the jury went across the street to examine a number of Whistler's pictures at the Westminster Palace Hotel. When the session was resumed, *The Falling Rocket* was shown to the jury and Sir John Holker began to question Whistler anew.

"This is Cremorne?" *(Laughter.)*

"It is a nocturne in black and gold," Whistler replied. Asked to explain the beauty of the picture, he went on: "It is as impossible for me to explain to you the beauty of that picture as it would be for a musician to explain to you the beauty of harmony in a particular piece of music if you had no ear for music."

"Do you not think Mr. Ruskin might have come to the conclusion that it had no particular beauty?"

"I think there is distinct evidence that he did. [Laughter.] I do not think that any artist would come to that conclusion."

After this stinging declaration Whistler's witnesses were called, starting with William Rossetti. As a friend of both Whistler and Ruskin, he was reluctant to testify. Of Whistler's works at the Grosvenor Gallery exhibit, he said, "Taking them altogether I admired them much, but not without exception." In what is certainly one of the oddest legal dialogues on record, Sir John then cross-examined Rossetti about *The Falling Rocket:* "Is it a gem?"

"No."

"Is it an exquisite painting?"

"No."

"Is it very beautiful?"

"No."

"Is it eccentric?"

"It is unlike the work of most other painters."

"Is it a work of art?"

"Yes, it is."

"Is two hundred guineas a stiffish price for a picture like that?"

"I think it is the full value of the picture." *(Laughter.)*

The visitors were ready to laugh at anything.

The critic John Ruskin, even as he attacks Whistler, is about to be stung by the scorpion tail of the artist's trademark, a butterfly, in this contemporary reference to the Whistler-Ruskin libel suit by the London cartoonist Phil May. Whistler is deceptively amiable in this caricature; it took him only a short time to file suit for £1,000 in damages after Ruskin, attacking a Whistler Nocturne, had charged in his magazine, *Fors Clavigera*, that the artist was "willful," "ill-educated" and impudent.

The next witness, the staunchly individualistic Albert Moore, pronounced Whistler's works "exquisite" and *The Falling Rocket* in particular a painting of "decided beauty." The last witness, a successful painter-playwright named William Gorman Wills, asserted that Whistler was a "genius" and his works "masterpieces."

For the defense the lead-off witness was Burne-Jones, who found *Battersea Bridge* "bewildering in its form." He was then asked whether *The Falling Rocket* was a finished work of art, and replied: "It would be impossible for me to say so. I have never seen any picture of night which has been successful; and this is only one of the thousand failures." Burne-Jones declared that *Rocket* was not worth 200 guineas, and then gratuitously added a cruel blow: "Mr. Whistler gave great promise at first, but I do not think he has fulfilled it."

The next Ruskin witness, William Powell Frith, took a crack at both *Battersea Bridge* and *The Falling Rocket*, testified that he was in court on subpoena and interjected that "it is a very painful thing to be called on to give evidence against a brother artist." Still, he seemed to be enjoying himself when Whistler's counsel, Serjeant Parry, asked if Frith would call Turner's *Snowstorm*, a powerful painting of a ship in the grip of a blizzard, "a mass of soapsuds and whitewash"—as a critic of Turner's time had labeled the work. Frith agreed: "I think it very likely I should. [Laughter.] When I say Turner should be the idol of everybody, I refer to his earlier works, and not to his later ones, which are as insane as the people who admire them." *(Laughter.)*

"Somebody," Judge Huddleston felt called upon to observe, "described one of Turner's pictures as 'lobster and salad.' "

"I have myself heard Turner speak of his own pictures as salad and mustard," Frith replied. *(Laughter.)*

"Without the lobster," Parry deadpanned. *(Laughter.)*

After this refreshing round of te-hees, Tom Taylor mounted the witness box as if it were a pulpit and quoted at considerable length from the gospel of his own articles in *The Times*, repeating that the Whistler paintings at issue came only "one step nearer to pictures than graduated tints on wallpaper."

In his charge to the jury the judge noted that "there are certain words by Mr. Ruskin about which . . . no one would entertain a doubt: those words amount to a libel. . . . The question for the jury is, did Mr. Whistler's ideas of art justify the language used by Mr. Ruskin? And the further question is whether the insult offered—if insult there has been—is of such a gross character as to call for substantial damages? Whether it is a case for merely contemptuous charges to the extent of a farthing . . . indicating that it is one which ought never to have been brought into court . . . or whether the case is one which calls for damages in some small sum as indicating the opinion of the jury that the offender has gone beyond the . . . letter of the law."

The jury, after an hour, gave the verdict to Whistler—but, following Judge Huddleston's thinly veiled suggestion, awarded him damages of only one farthing. His Lordship then disdainfully awarded judgment to Whistler "without costs"—meaning that even though

Voices in the Night.

First Voice:
"I am a Whistling devil-may-care,
  Nocturnally I go;
I paint me 'Harmonies' here and there,
  And hang them in a row.
Tol lol, tol lol, tol iddle, tol lol,
  I'd serve all the critics so."

Second Voice:
"I am a fiercely critical cuss,
  Despotic as Persian Shah;
And I used to kick up a bit of a fuss
  In my *Fors Clavigera*.
Tol lol, tol lol, tol iddle, tol lol,
  What coxcombs these painters are!"

Third Voice:
"I am the half of a halfpenny,
  Born in a melting pot;
And small as I be, you see, you see,
  A wonderful power I've got.
Tol lol, tol lol, tol iddle, tol lol,
  For I settled the blooming lot."

Ruskin had lost, he was not required to pay the expenses of the trial. He and Whistler were required to share them.

Whistler was determined to take the verdict as a moral victory. When a friend began to offer condolences, he broke in, "I was sure you would see what a great triumph it is!" Ruskin was equally determined to exaggerate his defeat. He resigned from the Slade Professorship at Oxford, saying that he could no longer hold a chair wherein he had "no power of expressing judgment without being taxed for it by British Law," woozily forgetting that he had not expressed his judgment from the Slade chair at all, but in his own widely read magazine, which had no link to his university position.

Superficially, the trial had an Alice-in-Wonderland quality, with prattle about mustard and lobster and a spurious jocularity throughout. But underneath, as Burne-Jones subsequently wrote to William Rossetti, "The whole thing was a hateful affair." It was galling for Whistler, who so painstakingly toiled over his works, to be accused of being slapdash. It was even more galling to be in a position where men ignorant of his esthetic aims had the power to humiliate him. Reporting on the trial for *The Nation*, Henry James called it "a singular and most regrettable exhibition. If it had taken place in some Western American town, it would have been called provincial and barbarous; it would have been cited as an incident of a low civilization. Beneath the stately towers of Westminster it hardly wore a higher aspect . . . the crudity and levity of the whole affair were decidedly painful."

James went on to say that Ruskin's language had transcended the decencies of criticism, and that for years the critic had indulged in "such promiscuous violence that it gratified one's sense of justice to see him brought up as a disorderly character . . . a general scold." James took occasion to reiterate that he himself did not care much for Whistler's art, except for the etchings, which he considered "altogether admirable."

To James, the trial was reprehensible largely on the grounds of bad

After a two-day trial a jury held that Ruskin had libeled Whistler and awarded him a farthing in damages, inspiring the cartoons shown here. Above, Whistler toots a penny whistle as an anonymous versifier-caricaturist makes the obvious pun on his name. Below, a *Punch* cartoon foreshadows the difficulties that the artist—drawn with penny-whistle legs and his distinctive lock of white hair—faced despite his victory: splitting court costs led to Whistler's bankruptcy.

AN APPEAL TO THE LAW.

When Whistler was forced to declare himself bankrupt in 1879 after the debacle and expenses of the Ruskin trial, notices *(above)* were posted in London announcing the auction of his one-year-old White House plus the artist's possessions. Whistler was scarcely resigned to the sale of his house and prized collections; he pettishly rejected as tasteless the phrase "On the Premises of Mr. Whistler" that appeared on the first printing of the notice *(below)*, and it was deleted on the final poster.

manners. Neither James nor anyone else could see, in 1878, that the trial was a landmark in the annals of art. What really was on trial was neither Ruskin nor Whistler, but an early manifestation of nonrepresentational art. By a hair, the defendant won. And the future lay open to an astonishing new era when unlimited freedom was to engulf the world of art, vastly stimulating it—if also often disorienting it.

With the trial behind him, Whistler faced problems more pressing than before it. While Ruskin's friends chipped in the necessary amount (about £385) to pay his half of the court costs, Whistler's friends were not similarly inspired. He was obliged to pay his half out of his own pocket, which was empty. His only possible solution was to declare bankruptcy. He had been broke before, but this was a grand crescendo of insolvency.

Even as the rituals of bankruptcy were being prepared, Whistler made his new White House more festive than ever, as if he were having the orchestra play while the ship was sinking. When a long-suffering frame maker was refused payment and instead was offered a glass of champagne, he protested: "You will pardon me, Mr. Whistler, but while you find yourself unable to settle my bill, I am surprised that you are able to indulge in the extravagance of champagne."

"Oh, don't let that worry you," was Whistler's reply. "I don't pay for that either."

And when he was besieged by bailiffs—whose fees were to be paid out of the money they collected from him—he cajoled them into putting on livery and serving at his fancy Sunday-morning breakfasts. "Your servants seem to be extremely attentive and anxious to please you," observed a lady guest. "Oh, yes," Whistler beamed at her. "I assure you they wouldn't leave." And when a particularly wretched bailiff complained after a week's service that his wife and children were penniless, Whistler brightly suggested that the man arrange to put a bailiff in his own house.

At times, however, his creditors outquipped him. When the secretary of the Arts Club, where Whistler had first read the Ruskin attack, dunned him for £30 in dues, Whistler suggested that in place of money the club might accept one of his paintings. The secretary retorted: "It is not a Nocturne in purple or a Symphony in blue and grey that we are after, but an Arrangement in gold and silver."

Of all historical documents, simple lists—of groceries, girls, bank deposits, anything—are sometimes the most touching. Whistler's list of debts at the end of his trial speaks volumes. He owed his fish dealer £97, his milkman £22, his oilman £136, his baker £12, his wine merchants £126. To a Chelsea builder he owed £60, to another in Lambert £226, to frame makers £86 and to his photographer £14.

In the West End he was in debt £20 to his tailor, £12 to his bootmaker, £27 to his shirtmaker. His lawyers' fees for the libel action amounted to almost £500. He borrowed lavishly from friends: £50 from W. C. Alexander, father of Cicely; £50 from Louis Huth, whose wife he had portrayed; £22 from his brother, William. Howell advanced £450, but held as security Whistler's portrait of his mother. In her nursing home in Hastings, Mrs. Whistler was mercifully spared these anxieties.

Bills announcing the sale of the White House, after Whistler had lived there less than a year, were pasted on his door. When they came loose and flapped untidily in the wind, Whistler insisted that they be pasted back *neatly*. For him, even the imminence of financial disaster had to be artistically arranged.

On May 8, 1879, Whistler announced himself bankrupt, with total assets amounting to £1,924 and debts to £4,641. A committee of creditors was formed and three examiners—Leyland, Howell and Thomas Way—were appointed. Whistler addressed them with a bitter speech excoriating the cupidity of the rich—aimed, of course, at Leyland, who proved, in part because of sums advanced Whistler on unfinished paintings, to be his largest creditor. But they did their best to help him. They arranged that his affairs be "liquidated"—meaning that his creditors could on their own release him from his debts, rather than letting him remain a declared bankrupt until the bankruptcy court saw fit to discharge him.

The examining trio had the painful duty of going to the White House to draw up an inventory of Whistler's possessions. In his studio they found three nasty caricatures of Leyland and the slashed remnants of several unfinished works that Whistler had decided to liquidate himself. The house and its contents were sold on September 18, 1879, for £2,700. The purchaser of the house was Harry Quilter, a well-known art critic whom Whistler had already chastised and subsequently teased and taunted by writing funny letters to the newspapers about him, referring to him always as 'Arry. Poor 'Arry, he might better have bought a house haunted by demons.

Increasingly, Whistler made belligerence a way of life. A few weeks after the trial, he had started publishing a series of pamphlets quoting his critics and adding his own tart retorts, thus always assuring himself the last word. Whistler was on his way to becoming an injustice collector. But it must be admitted that of all the many public figures who have kept scrapbooks about their activities, he was the only one who had the audacity to collect adverse criticism and reprint it in the conviction that future readers would find it as unjust and foolish as he did. On the whole Whistler has been proved right; the opinions of his detractors have not aged well.

Possessed of too much bile and too little money, Whistler faced an uneasy future. Providentially, he was rescued by London's Fine Art Society. Encouraged by its success in selling some of his etchings, the Society commissioned him to make 12 of Venice. He had planned repeatedly to go to that dream city but had never quite made it. Now was the ideal time to get out of London, forget the bailiffs and the bankruptcy. And Venice had a special lure for Whistler: it was on water. Throughout his life he had been attracted to water scenes, from New England to Russia to France and London. Now, for whatever injuries tormented him, Venice was offering him her water cure. A few days before the sale of the White House he left England for Italy.

The Gold Scab—Eruption in FRiLthy Lucre, a venomous caricature of Frederick R. Leyland complete with his capitalized initials and a pun on Leyland's love for frilly shirts, was painted by Whistler after he had been forced to declare himself bankrupt in 1879. Still irked by the old quarrel over the Peacock Room, Whistler had been further incensed to learn, after the bankruptcy proceedings, that his erstwhile patron was his principal creditor. In this, one of several Whistler lampoons of Leyland, the shipowner's skin is breaking out in golden scabs. He plays the piano while blithely perched atop Whistler's White House, which was sold to help liquidate his debts.

The famous controversy between Whistler and the art critic John Ruskin *(page 121)* was triggered by *The Falling Rocket,* a detail of which is shown opposite. The painting, along with several other Whistler Nocturnes and portraits, was displayed in an exhibition at London's fashionable Grosvenor Gallery in 1877. Before Ruskin's printed attack, Whistler's work had caused little stir at the show. As usual, some colleagues and reviewers tended to ignore his paintings, not certain of his artistic intent. Whistler's work was tolerated but the critical praise of the show was reserved for those who painted in a more recognizable style.

But Ruskin, the voice of tradition, the champion of carefully crafted art, saw nothing tolerable in Whistler's canvases. To him they seemed hurried, unfinished, chaotic, undistinguished by polish or intellectual purpose. Ruskin saw Whistler as nothing less than a self-promoting charlatan who was trying to sell slapdash paintings to an unwitting public as fine art.

Whistler ordinarily took criticism in stride, but Ruskin's attack was a deadly serious matter. For years the critic had been the dictator of English esthetic tastes. His disfavor meant loss of commissions, a cut in the prices a painter could charge and a drop in prestige in the closely knit English art world. Whistler, severely threatened by Ruskin's outburst, had no alternative: he immediately sued the critic for libel.

"A Pot of Paint"

Ruskin's charge that Whistler was merely "flinging a pot of paint in the public's face" is not hard to understand, as this detail shows. Seen at close range the spatterings and swirls of paint seem to have little form or meaning. Yet when the entire painting is examined *(overleaf)*, the work regains coherence and the sense of mood that Whistler worked so carefully to achieve.

Nocturne in Black and Gold: The Falling Rocket, detail, 1875

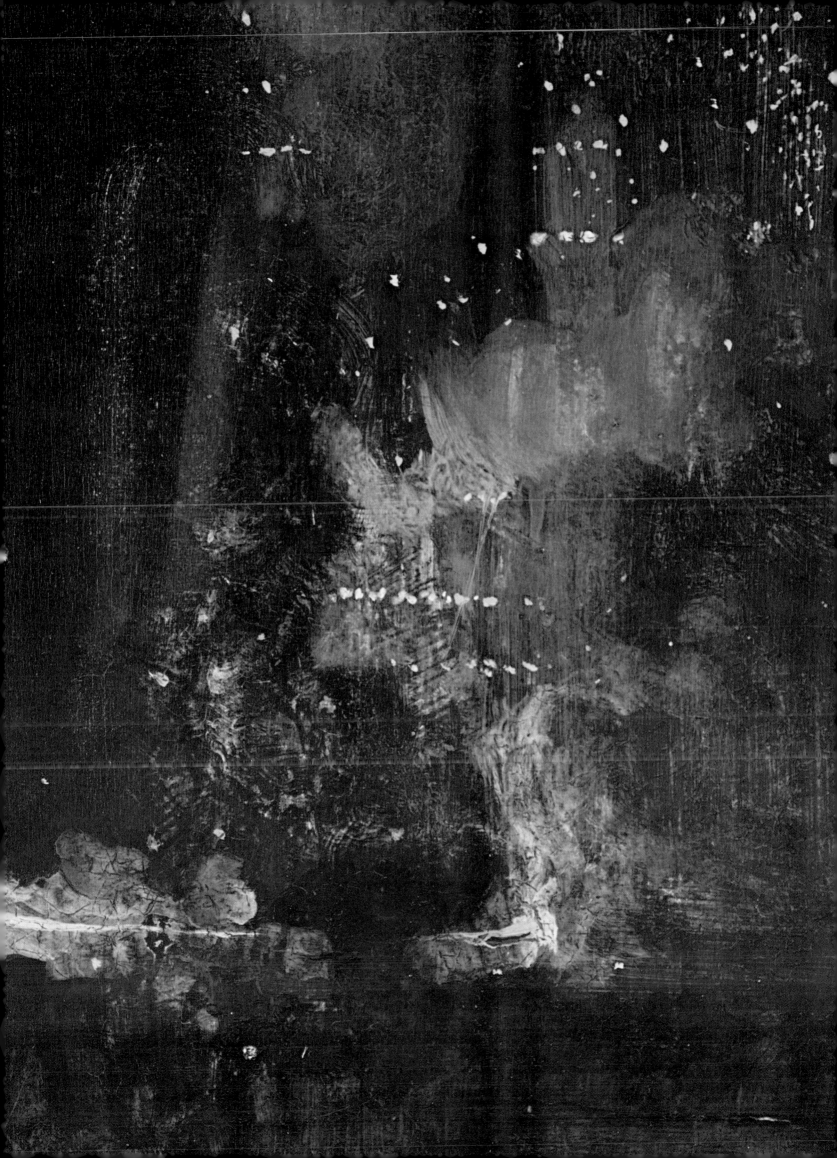

Nocturne in Black and Gold: The Falling Rocket, 1875

Whistler's Nocturnes, such as the two shown here, were simply meant to catch in color and tone the ambience of a nighttime scene. In fact, he originally called them "moonlights" until won over to the more poetic word "nocturne." *The Falling Rocket* is a study of fireworks bursting over one of London's most popular pleasure resorts, Cremorne Gardens. At the trial, Whistler tried in vain to explain this work. He begged the judge and jury not to regard it as a traditional painting that copied nature exactly but to view it instead as an "artistic arrangement." His case was not helped when the

134

Nocturne in Blue and Gold: Old Battersea Bridge, 1872-1875

painting was presented to the jury upside down.

The painting of *Old Battersea Bridge (above)* is clearer in its detail than *The Falling Rocket.* The view is down the Thames toward London. The ancient timber bridge towers above the water, a barge passes underneath, and glowing particles from skyrockets—a preview of the theme of the later painting—hang in the evening sky. It is a serene canvas that captures the lonely beauty of the hours of darkness. Yet so confounded was the judge by Whistler's style that he felt constrained to inquire of this painting: "The prevailing color is blue?"

Arrangement in Black No. 3: Sir Henry Irving, 1877

As with his Nocturnes, Whistler was forced to explain his wraithlike portraits to the courtroom. "All these works are impressions of my own," he said. "I make them my study. I suppose them to appeal to none but those who may understand the technical matter." Whether Whistler was understood or not, no viewer could doubt that the portraits are marked by the artist's unusual flair for the ethereal. In this study of his new mistress Maud Franklin, one of several portraits he painted of her, the darkened tone emphasizes the paleness of her face and gives the entire figure a gossamer appearance. Whistler's portrait of the actor Sir Henry Irving *(opposite)* is more robust. Shown dressed for his role as the Spanish monarch Philip II in Tennyson's *Queen Mary,* Irving stands sturdily, his eyes fixed on a distant point, his bearing and expression suggesting nobility. Straightforward as this portrait is, Whistler's title continued to confuse the court officials. "Why do you call Mr. Irving an *Arrangement in Black?*" the attorney general asked. When the judge, in perhaps the most sensible comment he made during the trial, pointed out to the lawyer that the painting, not Mr. Irving, was the *arrangement,* the courtroom rocked with laughter.

Arrangement in Black and Brown: The Fur Jacket, 1870s

137

In the carnival air that pervaded the courtroom, Whistler's art had little chance of being taken seriously. He won the case, but the jury awarded only the smallest token payment—one farthing. Whistler promptly claimed a moral victory. He had the farthing mounted on his watch chain and wore it proudly.

Thereafter, undaunted by the skeptical attitude of critics and public alike, he continued painting and exhibiting his controversial Nocturnes. One of his finest *(right)* was shown at the same Grosvenor Gallery just a year after the trial. A view of London's Chelsea section from across the Thames, it is a stunning example of Whistler's genius for creating mood through the blending of soft hues. His Nocturnes, no matter how misunderstood at the time, illustrate what the artist once wrote to his friend Fantin-Latour. "Color ought to be, as it were, embroidered on the canvas . . . the same color ought to appear in the picture continually here and there, in the same way that a thread appears in an embroidery . . . in this way, the whole will form a harmony."

Nocturne in Blue and Green: Chelsea, 1871

VII

Veneration in Venice

For quick sketches in intense colors, pastel has always been a medium favored by artists. Whistler took it up in Venice, where he had gone to do a series of etchings for an English publisher. His method was to outline the main details of his subject in black crayon on tinted paper and then fill in patches of pure color with mosaiclike care. As in the pastel shown here, the technique looks easy; Whistler wryly agreed that "only the doing it was the difficulty."

Alley in Venice, 1880

After the debacle of the Ruskin trial, Venice restored Whistler's spirits, providing him with new admirers and followers and fresh material for the exercise of his talent and the honing of his engraving skills. But in the fall of 1879 the London wounds still hurt. In his Venice rooms he hung a photograph of his caricature of Leyland as a grasping bird. And as if to keep the wounds fresh, he regaled his new friends with details of the case, going over and over the stupidities of Ruskin's spokesmen and his own brilliant comebacks.

One day he impaled a scorpion on his etching needle, and as the insect fought to escape, kicking out desperately with its legs, Whistler cried, "Look at the beggar now! See him strike! Hit hard! Do you see the poison that comes out when he strikes? Isn't he superb?" Whistler clearly identified himself with his venomous victim, and the scorpion's barbed tail began to appear in his official butterfly signature.

Part of Whistler's outrageousness, of course, was pure exuberance, something irrepressibly Barnum-like that balanced the introverted side of an artist whose work was essentially quiet and withdrawn. Indeed, his psychological well-being depended on keeping these opposite sides in equilibrium. But, since the Ruskin trial, the need to justify and advertise himself threatened to destroy his balance. At times it seemed questionable whether he could survive his own animosities. In Venice the answer was pending.

He took an instant liking to the city. Venice, he wrote, was "an impossible place to sit down and sketch. There was always something far better just around the corner." And indeed Venice offered Whistler boundless possibilities. But he rejected most of its celebrated sights —the Rialto, the Grand Canal, the Piazza di San Marco—in favor of hidden courtyards, alleys, small bridges. He had resolved that the set of 12 etchings ordered by the London Fine Art Society would not be a cliché-ridden collection of Venetian landmarks.

At first he settled in rooms at the Palazzo Rezzonico on the Grand Canal. But he disliked the Palazzo's red brocade walls and its gloomy courtyard; soon he moved to humbler quarters on the edge of Venice's slums, where he was joined by Maud Franklin, who came from London to cook, housekeep and enliven his poverty. Still, he was lonesome for London. Like an actor deprived of stage and audience, he missed having servants to order around. His valet, his models, his maid, his devoted young hangers-on like the Greaves brothers were as necessary to him as pages and courtiers to a prince. He made friends, to be sure, with the American consul, a Mr. Grist, and he frequented the English Club. But for a while things did not go well.

One of the last photographs made of Whistler was taken in the 1890s in his Paris studio on the Rue Notre-Dame-des-Champs as he stood beside his etching press. The largest studio the artist ever used, it had room not only for a small but complete printing shop but also for several easels, plus storage space for canvases, a print cabinet and a model's dressing room. As always, however, Whistler kept the studio sparsely decorated.

It was the coldest winter in 30 years. He shivered on his sketching trips, and the copper plates on which he made his etchings were like slabs of ice in his hands. He was slow in getting to work. The Fine Art Society had specified when Whistler left London in September that it wanted the plates for its 12 etchings delivered by mid-December, and it gave him an advance on the promised fee of £1,200. When weeks passed without word from Whistler the Society wrote to demand an explanation. The answer was silence, and then Whistler wrote to ask for more money. To his enemies this was proof that Whistler was out to squeeze all the cash he could get from the Society, with no intention of delivering on the commission. But he did eventually get down to work, although no one knows quite when; presumably at some point he mollified the secretary of the Fine Art Society with a report that the assignment was underway.

A fortunate event was his meeting with a group of young American art students, including one in particular, Otto Bacher, who had studied his etchings. Bacher, who later wrote a book about Whistler in Venice, recalled that he first saw the artist with Consul Grist near the Academy of Fine Arts. Whistler, Bacher wrote, was a "curious, sailor-like stranger," with broad-brimmed hat tilted back to show his white lock. "These are all American boys," said Grist, and then turned to the students. "Boys, let me introduce you to Mr. Whistler."

"Whistler is charmed," the stranger repeated as he shook hands with each. When he came to Bacher, the consul broke in. "Mr. Whistler, this is the boy who etches."

"Ah, indeed! Whistler is quite charmed and will be glad to see your work." It is hard to say precisely why Whistler referred to himself in the third person. Surely he knew the mannerism appeared insufferably pompous. But after the humiliation of the trial and his bankruptcy, he doubtless felt like flaunting his self-esteem, impudently, defiantly, as much as to say: If the world won't speak my name with awe and deference, at least I will; and though you may suspect I am being funny, I dare you to laugh at me. Nobody did.

Meeting young Bacher again at a dinner given by Grist, Whistler was eager to know what kind of press he used. How large an etching plate could it accommodate? After learning that it was a fine German press, Whistler asked if Bacher had any German-made ink. When Bacher said he had, Whistler replied, "Good," and then, as if conferring a royal boon, added, "I will come and try your ink and press, and take a look at . . . the prints you have of mine."

Whistler did not move with undue haste. A month passed before he called on Bacher and his crew at the Casa Jacovitz, a sort of Venetian rooming house with a view across open water of the Doge's Palace. Bacher was studying with a gifted American teacher and painter, Frank Duveneck, who had been trained in Munich and whose pupils, tagging him around Europe, were known as "Duveneck's Boys." They welcomed Whistler. And he, in turn, so enjoyed the view, the press, the ink and the quarters that he moved into the Casa Jacovitz.

Working at last, Whistler rented a gondola with a handsome old gondolier named Calvadora. The artist left his copper plates in the bottom of the boat, protected between the leaves of a book. In his pockets he kept his etching needles—ordinary dentist's tools.

When he etched, Whistler usually grasped the wax-coated copper plate in his left hand and, holding the needle in the other, sketched away through the wax with ease and fluency, as if using pencil on paper. Bacher observed: "He grouped his lines in an easy, playful way that was fascinating; they would often group themselves as tones, a difficult thing to get in an etching."

Bacher especially admired Whistler's ability to suggest the deep tones of open doorways and cool courtyards in contrast to the Adriatic sunlight, and to hint at the presence of forms almost concealed in the shadows. "He worked for hours on figures, and at times became quite excited . . . 'Look at this figure!' he yelled to me one day. 'See how well he stands!' "

Whistler's earlier etchings—*The French Set* and the Thames series—had been magnificent, but he was now surpassing himself. He revealed a fresh vision of Venice, a city that in the past had been extravagantly over-painted—and under-etched. Artists in general had felt that Venice, at least the Venice everybody knew, was so gloriously pigmented that it was mandatory to show it in full color. In defiance of this, Whistler selected his personal Venice, and made it a monochrome city of intimate passageways and enchanting shadows, sites and scenes little known to tourists or doges—and most of them unrecognizable even to the most assiduous art scholar. Even now no one quite knows the precise location of *The Mast (page 158)*, an intimate study of a small square in which Venetians chat before a soaring flagpole. It is conceivable that Whistler transported the mast from another setting —similar ones stud the Piazza di San Marco—and placed it in his engraved square for purposes of composition: the mast and its lanyards effectively frame the gesticulating Venetians. Similarly, the location of *The Traghetto No. 2 (The Ferry, pages 158-159)* is unknown. It is but one of the innumerable places along the canals of the city where citizens awaited the boats that served as buses. It is not even clear from the etching what the waiting passengers—or dock hands—are doing. Seated at a table before a shadowed archway, they play cards or drink or roll dice, and what they are up to does not matter. As always, Whistler was in search of atmosphere, not anecdotage.

All together, he produced more than 40 etched plates of Venetian views. *The French Set* and the Thames work alone would have assured him a place among the world's finest etchers; the Venice series established him in the front rank. His approach in all of the plates was peculiarly personal. "I began first of all," he once remarked, "by seizing upon the chief point of interest . . . perhaps it might have been the extreme distance—the little palaces and shipping beneath the bridge. If so, I would begin drawing that distance in elaborately, and then would expand from it until I came to the bridge, which I would draw in one broad sweep. If by chance I did not see the whole bridge, I would not put it in." In other words, Whistler emphasized and developed exactly what caught his eye, near or far, and slighted whatever seemed to him of lesser importance.

Aside from some pleasing watercolors, Whistler made very few paintings in Venice. But he developed considerable skill with pastels —concentrating, again, on muted, suggestive street scenes, as in *Alley in Venice (page 140)*. On a pastel expedition he always carried two boxes of the colored chalks in his gondola, one filled with broken bits of odd colors for the early skirmishes and another of new, unused pieces for the final work. He also kept a supply of colored papers —pinks, tans, blues, according to the background tone he wanted.

To begin a pastel, he chose his ready-made background, then outlined his subject neatly in black. Finally, he touched in colors here and there: architectural details, balconies, windows, chimney pots, boats. He turned out more than 50 of these pastel impressions. They were clues to color, shorthand notes, memos and innuendoes of color rather than full statements, yet they were powerful evocations of the multihued city. As always, Whistler enjoyed creating the contrast between atmospheric skies and clean-cut architecture, and delighted in capturing the elusive effect of reflections in water.

Basking in the admiration of Bacher and the rest of Duveneck's Boys, turning out work that his own eye told him was superb, he gradually found that the London wounds no longer throbbed so fiercely. As his spirits were restored, he returned to the prankishness of his student days. When he saw one of Ruskin's friends sketching a detail of a mosaic in the Cathedral of San Marco, Whistler hastily lettered the words "I Am Totally Blind" on a sheet from his sketch pad, crept up behind the man and pinned it on his coattail. The innocent sketcher was soon astonished to find himself the center of a fascinated crowd.

Like all sojourners in Venice, Whistler spent part of his days sitting at the little tables outside the Café Florian or the Quadri in the Piazza di San Marco; he listened to the band playing in the square and lifted his monocle to stare or nod at such visitors as Franz Liszt, George Eliot, Richard Wagner, or his fellow American and incipient rival, the young painter John Singer Sargent. Although most people who knew Whistler in Venice enjoyed his company, one sour note was struck by Henry Woods, an English artist who kept up a running account of Whistler in his letters home. "Whistler, I hear, has been borrowing money from everybody, and from some who can ill afford to spare it . . . he is the cheekiest scoundrel out." Bacher, the American art student, told a different story about Whistler's scrounging, declaring that he "rarely ever asked the other boys for money; on one occasion in returning a borrowed sum he insisted on giving me twice as much."

In November 1880 Whistler returned to London, unannounced, and hurried to make a grand entrance at a Fine Art Society exhibition, holding in one hand an extra-long cane and with the other leading on a ribbon a white Pomeranian dog. Unmistakably the show was on.

"As I walked in," he recalled later, "I spoke to no one, but putting up my glass I looked at the prints on the wall. 'Dear me, dear me!' I said, 'still the same old sad work! Dear me!' "

Whistler had good reason to be in high spirits. He had brought back from Venice not only 40 superb etchings—from which the pleased Fine Art Society selected the 12 it had commissioned—but the magnificently evocative pastels that he had executed out of his own artistic impulse. Moreover, he was about to become a father again; Maud was now awaiting the birth of their child in Paris.

Regrettably, however, the etchings did not prove an instant success. The 12 chosen by the Fine Art Society were shown at its Bond Street gallery in December, and the critics, echoing the old charge that his work was "unfinished," castigated them as "another crop of Whistler's little jokes." But, paradoxically, the pastels were a different matter. Like the engravings, they were impressions of mood, equally "unfinished." Yet, when they were exhibited a month after the engravings, also at the Fine Art gallery, they were a rousing success. Maud, mother of a brand-new daughter, reported to Bacher that the show was "very fashionable." During the preview, sidewalks were jammed and Bond Street was choked with carriages. Perhaps the explanation for the pastels' acceptance lies in the fact that John Millais —by now a knight as well as a member of the Royal Academy and a most successful Establishment painter—loved them. He roared through the gallery, bellowing, "Magnificent . . . very cheeky, but fine." In any event, Whistler received £1,800 from the sale of pastels and was at last restored to solvency.

There was, however, a sad note in this hour of triumph. While the show was still in progress, Whistler received an urgent summons from his younger brother, Dr. William Whistler, who was attending their mother in her Hastings nursing home. She had been in poor health for years, but her death, at age 74, on January 31, 1881, came unexpectedly. After the funeral, Whistler walked the Sussex moors with his brother, despairingly crying, "It would have been much better had I been a parson as she wanted." This was nonsense, of course. Anna Mathilda Whistler had a far more exciting life as the mother of Jimmy Whistler, the expatriate artist, than she would have had as the mother of Parson Whistler of Stonington, Connecticut. And she would not have attained immortality as the mother image of a nation.

Within the year, Whistler's *Mother* actually reached the United States. At the urging of the Pennsylvania Academy of Fine Arts, Whistler sent the portrait over for an exhibit; it was the first time he had ever been represented in his native country. A few months later *Mother* was shown in New York. But no American bought it. The Americans' lack of appreciation galled Whistler; when he was later asked why he never visited the U.S., he explained: "It has been suggested many times, but you see I find art so absolutely irritating to the people that, really, I hesitate before exasperating another nation."

Soon after his mother's death he moved into 13 Tite Street, not far from the White House. His old home was still occupied by the much-maligned 'Arry Quilter, a situation that moved Whistler to remark, "Shall the birthplace of art become the tomb of a parasite?" It was but one of a number of malicious cracks he began to make. Whistler was back in stride. He filled the newspapers with letters, resumed his Sunday breakfasts and took to dressing, if possible, more eccentrically than before. His cane lengthened and pink bows sprouted on his black shoes. He wanted the town to talk about him—and it did.

In 1883 Whistler put on a larger show of his Venetian etchings, and this time the fashionable people of London flocked in to view the works of eccentric Mr. Whistler as if they were going to a garden party. Whistler adorned the gallery in yellow and gave away silk butterflies as souvenirs; he realized that his success was as much due to showmanship as to art, and he was hell-bent to make the most of it. He escorted the Prince of Wales around the gallery at the private showing, and when somebody told him later that the Prince had mentioned knowing Mr. Whistler, it amused him to answer, "That's only his side."

Now he resolved to build up his resources by painting portraits of the fashionable, a perfectly feasible idea except that Whistler did not have the temperament for it. He took too long and bullied his subjects, and the results lacked the flashy craftsmanship that flattered the average sitter. He did entice into his studio a few prominent subjects who were willing to put up with him—to a point.

He worked on three portraits of Lady Meux, a dark beauty with fiery eyes. The first was an *Arrangement in White and Black*, showing her regally attired in a velvet cloak. In the second, *Harmony in Flesh Color and Pink: Valerie, Lady Meux (page 178)*, he created a luscious blending of silvery grays and pink, dashed with blue. It is saved from overdelicacy by the passages of thick pigment slapped on the bustle and on the low-brimmed hat, beneath which Lady Meux peers out like a sassy black kitten in a pale-pink rose garden.

During the painting of the third portrait, Whistler at one point spoke sharply to her. "See here, Jimmy Whistler," she answered with claws in her voice, "you keep a civil tongue in that head of yours, or I will have in someone to *finish* those portraits you made of me." Whistler, stung by the old implication that his work was unfinished, howled with rage. "How dare you? How dare you?" he cried, holding his brush tight to his side to keep from striking her. Lady Meux left at once and never returned—and the third portrait was, indeed, unfinished.

Lady Archibald Campbell, during one of the countless sittings for a portrait, became so upset at something Whistler said that she ran out to her carriage and was persuaded to return only when a friend suggested to her that she was depriving the world of a masterpiece. He eventually did two portraits of her, but destroyed one (which she thought was already "a masterpiece") when she had to leave town be-

Often caricatured by others, Whistler poked fun at himself in this drawing showing him working on three portraits simultaneously. The cartoon is close to the truth, however. He did indeed work on three portraits of a wealthy society woman, Lady Meux, and he did lunge at his canvases, fencer style, with inordinately long brushes. Only two of the three portraits, one of which is shown on page 178, were finished; after a quarrel with the artist, Lady Meux refused to finish sitting for the third.

fore the final sitting. He relegated the task of destruction to a young disciple, Walter Sickert, after much indecision. According to Sickert's account, one evening before the two of them went out for dinner Whistler stood on a chair holding a candle, trying to decide whether to wipe out the portrait. Not until they were in the street did he make up his mind. "You go back," Whistler said. "I shall only be nervous and begin to doubt again." Sickert obeyed, effacing the work with a rag and benzine. Such caprices did not endear Whistler to ladies of fashion.

Whistler had less trouble with a portrait of Théodore Duret, a Parisian journalist, politician and art critic who was an intimate of Manet and Fantin-Latour. Whistler's French friends had a calming effect on him; they were bored by his showing-off and impressed by his merits. ("You behave," Degas told him, "as if you had no talent.") Whistler portrayed Duret, who visited London often on business, as if he were returning from a ball, dressed formally in black but holding a red fan *(page 179)*. Although Whistler repainted the portrait 10 times, Duret endured the ordeal patiently because the interminable sittings gave him an insight into the artist's theories and methods.

He reported that Whistler began work by marking lightly with chalk the exact location of the figure on the canvas, then brushed in all the colors so that by the end of the first sitting the whole color scheme was displayed. Whistler started all over again when dissatisfied because he felt that simple retouching seldom helped to achieve the effect of perfect unity that he was seeking.

Whistler's portraits in this period are among his finest works. To be sure, they lack the freshness of the *Cicely Alexander, Mother* and *Carlyle* portraits. But they possess an extra, mysterious authority, perhaps indicating that the artist had at last reached a maturity and balance, that the sojourn in Venice and the subsequent successes had given him an equanimity reflected in his work.

Still, he was not part of the contemporary stream, as he never would be. In art circles the moralizing aspect of the early Pre-Raphaelites had fallen out of style, making room for a new phenomenon loosely called Estheticism. It took its roots from a variety of sources, most conspicuous among them being the English critic Walter Pater, who believed that life should be an attempt to experience moments of "exquisite awareness." A man should "burn always with this hard, gem-like flame," Pater wrote, spending his days in "high passions," the best of which were "art and song." At first hearing, this sounded like Whistler's old battle cry, Art for Art's Sake, and, indeed, the followers of the Esthetic Movement adopted many of Whistler's mannerisms and interests. They were given to eccentricity in dress, favoring loose, flowing costumes, and they betrayed a passion for Oriental art, particularly Chinese porcelain. But Whistler never became a part of the cult, which was essentially a shallow reaction against Victorian prudery, assuming forms that were fey and flighty. Nevertheless, he became identified with Estheticism in the public mind—a circumstance that eventually annoyed him and led him to make a public declaration of his own gemlike dedication to the muse of art.

PUNCH PUBLICATIONS LTD., LONDON

THE SIX-MARK TEA-POT.

Æsthetic Bridegroom. "It is quite consummate, is it not!"
Intense Bride. "It is, indeed! Oh, Algernon, let us live up to it!"

Spoofing the Esthetic Movement, this cartoon by du Maurier satirizes the craze for Chinese porcelain—also joshed in the verses below from the operetta *Patience.*

*Come, walk up, and purchase with
    avidity,
Overcome your diffidence and natural
    timidity,
Tickets for the raffle should be
    purchased with avidity,
        Put in half a guinea and a husband
        you may gain—
Such a judge of blue-and-white and
    other kinds of pottery—
From early Oriental down to modern
    terra-cotta-ry—
Put in half a guinea—you may draw him
    in a lottery—
        Such an opportunity may not occur
        again.*

The most conspicuous of the new esthetes was a young Irishman named Oscar Fingal O'Flahertie Wills Wilde, son of Sir William and Lady Wilde. After three years at Trinity College, Dublin, Wilde had entered Oxford and in 1877 had dropped down to London to review for a Dublin periodical the famous Grosvenor Gallery exhibit that led to the Whistler-Ruskin trial. To Wilde, Whistler's *Falling Rocket*, the picture that precipitated the whole affair, was "worth looking at for about as long as one looks at a real rocket, that is, for something less than a quarter of a minute." Apparently, Whistler had never read Wilde's comment, for after meeting him at a reception he invited him to a Sunday breakfast and eventually took him on as one of his disciples. Twenty years younger than the master, Oscar Wilde was an admiring and amusing satellite, kinder by nature than Whistler and better educated. Wilde, the languid giant, and Whistler, the gingery dwarf, made a dazzling team at social gatherings, a sort of esthetic Mutt and Jeff. "There was something about both of them," wrote the actress Ellen Terry, "more instantaneously individual and audacious than it is possible to describe."

There was also something about both of them, different as they were, that epitomized the Esthetic Movement in the public mind. The blue-and-white china that Whistler collected and the languorous posing of Wilde were satirized at length in *Punch*, whose brilliant staff cartoonist, George du Maurier, became the chief fun-poker at esthetic goings on in the 1880s. Although the movement had been simmering for some time, it burst on the English public around 1880 when du Maurier produced a cartoon gallery that included Mrs. Cimabue Brown, who was mad for Chinese pottery; Jellaby Postlethwaite, said to be a take-off of Wilde; and the Jack Spratts, an artistic couple who gushed about such imaginary early Italian painters as Antima Cassaro and Fra Stoggiato di Vermicelli. And because Wilde was rumored to have walked down Piccadilly holding a lily—the esthetes were much taken with flowers—there were several du Maurier caricatures of men and women spending their mealtime in deep contemplation of a single flower. Du Maurier noted, in one cartoon, that the Esthetic Movement was "too utterly utter."

But the esthetic lunacy got its most memorable lampooning in the Gilbert and Sullivan comic operetta *Patience, or Bunthorne's Bride*, produced in London in 1881. The poetic hero, Bunthorne, who had 20 maidens swooning with unrequited passion, was a composite of Wilde and Whistler. With a monocle and white forelock bobbing from a mop of unruly hair, Bunthorne so closely resembled the American painter that the composer, Sir Arthur Sullivan, stopped in Whistler's box at the theater to apologize for the likeness.

After the success of *Patience* at the new Savoy Theater, where electric lights were used for the first time on an English stage, the operetta was produced in New York. Because it was not well received at first, its producer suggested that Wilde make a lecture tour to America during the show's run to help boost business. Wilde had no interest in promoting *Patience*, but he liked the suggestion of an American tour. He traveled to the U.S. in 1882 and gave 90 lectures, including one in Boston, where the hall was filled with Harvard boys, each sporting a lily in his buttonhole and carrying a sunflower. The success of Wilde's tour (he talked on "Home Decoration" and "The English Renaissance") did not endear him to Whistler, who was sure he had taught Wilde nearly everything he knew, or thought he knew, about art. In fact, Whistler was harboring a burgeoning resentment against Wilde on grounds that the writer was poaching on the artist's intellectual preserve. Whistler's best-known witticism reflected this feeling. It was delivered just after he had made some quip and Wilde had exclaimed: "I wish I had said that." Whistler's answer was: "You will, Oscar, you will."

This was no casual crack; Whistler really believed that Wilde was plagiarizing his ideas. For example, one of Whistler's most deeply felt precepts was that nature in her raw and unruly state had no value for artists. He had absorbed this notion years ago from Gautier and Baudelaire, but he had applied it specifically to painting, and now he claimed it with some justice as his property. The only countryside that he did not find detestable was that of Holland, where "the trunks of the trees are painted white, the cows wear quilts." He even criticized evenings on the Thames, which he really loved. When a disciple risked saying, "The stars are fine tonight," Whistler grumbled: "Not bad, but there are too many of them."

In short, it was the artist's job to select and rearrange what he wanted from nature, and any idiot who tried to represent the whole caboodle, he said, was like a musician sitting on the piano keys.

Beyond doubt, Wilde had assimilated and expanded Whistler's doctrine in his essay "The Decay of Lying," in which he proclaimed the superiority of art to nature in his famous paradox, "Nature imitates Art." To Whistler this was galling; he was, after all, already on record as having remarked to a lady who told him that the exquisite morning mist on the Thames reminded her of his art, "Yes, Madam, Nature is creeping up."

The hostility between Whistler and Wilde was fanned by certain London papers, which made it a practice to egg well-known people to write one another nasty letters, which were then printed for the public's delectation. These two brilliant men, each huffing to be funnier and deadlier than the other, conducted a verbal slugfest in the press that was worthy of neither and that grew increasingly painful to watch.

But despite their foolishness both the combatants benefited. Wilde learned from Whistler, and Whistler was stung by Wilde's success as a public speaker to crystallize his theories on art and beat Oscar at his own game. He too would lecture in public. To advise him, Whistler recruited an acquaintance, Mrs. Richard D'Oyly Carte, who was a producer for Gilbert and Sullivan. She helped him hire a hall, prepare tickets and listened to him rehearse his lecture—called "The Ten O'Clock" to advertise to the members of his fashionable audience that he would not start talking until they had finished their after-dinner port at leisure. In a sense Whistler had always been on stage. Now he was creeping up on himself.

Modeled after Whistler and Oscar Wilde, the protagonist of W. S. Gilbert's libretto for *Patience* is the effete poet Reginald Bunthorne *(above)*, mocked in Gilbert's verse below.

BRITISH MUSEUM, LONDON

If you walk down Piccadilly with a
*   poppy or a lily in your medieval hand,*
And everyone will say,
As you walk your flowery way,
"If he's content with a vegetable love
*   which would certainly not suit me,*
Why, what a particularly pure young
*   man this pure young man must be!"*

The Favorite Etchings

Etching was the first art form that Whistler mastered, and he remained lastingly devoted to it. Much of his reputation as a major artist is owed to the prints he produced, and to the superb technique and remarkably fresh vision they reveal. Scholars and critics sometimes compare them to the etchings of no less a titan than Rembrandt, whose scenes of Holland have their equivalent in Whistler's studies of London and Venice.

When it came to choosing subjects for his etcher's eye, Whistler scorned both the picturesque and the commonplace. In an early series known as "The Thames Set" he explored the grimy London waterfront and transformed dockside chaos into a world of precise harmonies. Later, in Venice, he ignored the tourist landmarks and instead prowled the quieter canals for evocative studies of light and shadow on water. And when his etching needle scratched the human figure into a copper plate, he achieved a fullness and a sense of dimension with the merest suggestion of line and texture. The rich white of the paper he used—he especially loved old paper, for its mellow tone—says as much as the black of his inked line.

For an exhibition of his etchings at the Columbian Exposition of 1893 in Chicago Whistler was asked to select works he judged his finest. The prints on the following pages, presented in roughly chronological order, are among the personal favorites he chose.

Whistler once said that he would be willing to stake his name as an etcher on this portrait of his niece, Annie Haden; he even wrote in the lower right-hand corner, "one of my very best." The contrast between the girl's delicate beauty and the dark background is achieved with utmost economy. The sophisticated simplification of this early work characterizes Whistler's best efforts.

Annie Haden, 1860 (13¾″ × 8⅜″)

Becquet, c. 1860 (actual size)

Axenfeld, 1860 (actual size)

The Kitchen, 1858 (actual size)

The Lime-burner, c. 1860 (actual size)

Black Lion Wharf, 1859 (5⅞″ × 8⅞″)

Whistler: 1859.

The Mast, c. 1880 (13⅜″ × 6⁷/₁₆″)

The Traghetto No. 2, c. 1880 (actual size)

The Palaces, c. 1880 (actual size)

The Smithy, early 1880s (6⅞″ × 9″)

THE SMITHSONIAN INSTITUTION, FREER GALLERY OF ART, WASHINGTON, D.C.

The Embroidered Curtain, 1889 (actual size)

The Long House—Dyer's—Amsterdam, c. 1889 (6½″ × 10⁹⁄₁₆″)

166

VIII

"Art for Art's Sake"

Prince's Hall in Piccadilly, where Whistler early in 1885 delivered his definitive artistic credo, "The Ten O'Clock" lecture, had housed various attractions, from Negro minstrel shows to symphony concerts, giving the place a catholic ambience well suited to Whistler himself. Walking on stage before his audience, which had gathered at the fashionable after-dinner hour of 10 o'clock, he reminded some of its members of an elegant conjurer as he leaned his cane against a wall, set his opera hat on a table and deftly shed his gloves. Dressed in formal black, and standing against a black background, he was a study in black on black, relieved only by his white shirt.

"Ladies and Gentlemen: It is with great hesitation and much misgiving that I appear before you, in the character of The Preacher."

From the start, he surprised his audience with his gravity. No jokes, no invective. To one observer Whistler seemed to offer little that he had not already said at countless dinner tables. This was mainly true. But now he had organized and polished his thoughts into a manifesto for posterity.

The total effect of the speech was to affirm the exclusivity of art and artists, to set them apart from the crowd, subject to their own laws and responsible only to themselves. He declared that art, like a loose woman, had been on the town, cheapened by too much intimacy with the public, "chucked under the chin by the passing gallant." He lashed out, as he had before, against critics and do-gooders who demanded that art should be preachy. He stated that only other artists were qualified to criticize art, and he took an extra swipe at his old foe Ruskin by asserting that artists were a dedicated priesthood, joyous in the service of their goddess, with no need whatsoever of babbling critics.

He also put Nature in her place. Nature, he charged, was "casual," a producer of "foolish sunsets." She was useful to artists, yes, as source material. But her works needed to be edited in the studio. For all his deification of art, Whistler kept a tough-minded attitude toward his goddess. The arts, he felt, should not be coddled and gushed over, but should be taken for granted. He declared, moreover, that beauty

167

dwelled not only in the past, but in all times. "Why this lifting of the brow," he challenged, "in deprecation of the present?"

Whistler's lecture contained one reckless statement. In his eagerness to affirm the independence of art, he denied that art was in any way influenced or shaped by historical circumstances. The great artist, he insisted, "stands in no relation to the moment in which he occurs . . . having no part in the progress of his fellow men. Art happens. . . . Art we in no way affect."

The lecture left its audience curiously soothed. It took Art off their backs, absolving them of any obligation to worry over her. Foreseeably, the speech found less favor with the critics. Oscar Wilde objected to the dictum that art is unaffected by history, and bristled at the idea that only painters were fit to criticize painting. But he ended with a salute to Whistler, albeit with a final tweak: "That he is indeed one of the very greatest masters of painting is my opinion. And I may add that, in this opinion, Mr. Whistler himself entirely concurs."

Despite such criticism "The Ten O'Clock" was a significant document in the history of art. It reflected a major change in the artist's role in society, a change that became conspicuous during Whistler's day and extends into modern times. The artist, to a greater extent than ever before, had begun to think of himself as an outsider. With the dwindling importance of church and monarchy, he was less and less needed to glorify these ancient institutions. His contribution to the world was no longer a vital necessity. He was expendable. To adjust to this crisis, many men of art chose to believe not that society had rejected them, but that they had rejected society. In Whistler's case this resulted in an ambivalent urge to defy the world he most desired.

The artist's age-old impulse to flaunt his individuality, moreover, was suddenly intensified by new threats, new omens. The doctrines of Marx and Darwin, and later of Freud, provided a new deterministic view of the world, wherein effect followed cause, it seemed, in soulless lock step. The artist saw still another threat to Art in the drab conformity of mass production, in the mercantile mentality. So now, more than ever, Art must remain defiantly free. Dispossessed by the past and distrustful of the present, the artist must learn to survive alone —and like it. This was the burden of Whistler's "Ten O'Clock" lecture, the historical crisis that had set him shouting, as if he were leading a cavalry charge, "Art for Art's Sake!"

With this statement of his artistic credo at maturity, Whistler entered the final two decades of his life. It was not for him a notably productive period, but rather a time of benefits reaped from his earlier efforts. He was held in higher esteem. Ironically, despite his belief that there never was an art-loving period, honors poured in on him from all over Europe and, more cautiously, from America. Gradually but increasingly accepted as a man of genius, he won medals, held prestigious positions, worked at what he liked—mainly small paintings and etchings—and, at last, made a wonderful marriage. And just to keep himself in trim he engaged in a few rip-roaring feuds.

The success of "The Ten O'Clock" lecture brought eight invitations to repeat his speech under auspices varying from university groups at Oxford and Cambridge to a somewhat fuddy-duddy London organization called the Society of British Artists and even—in the heart of enemy territory—the Royal Academy Students' Club. His prestige was growing, especially among the young.

In 1884, a year before the lecture, Whistler had been visited by a deputation of younger members from the British Artists, who felt they needed new life in their venerable Suffolk Street mansion. When invited to join the Society, Whistler was probably as dumfounded as the London *Times* man, who wrote, "Artistic society was startled by the news that this most wayward, most un-English of painters had found a home among the men of Suffolk Street, of all people in the world!" And even more startling, after the original "Ten O'Clock" talk, Whistler was elected president of the club.

He delighted the older members by cajoling a royal charter out of Queen Victoria by sending her an "Address" on the 50th anniversary of her coronation in 1887. Painted by himself, on sheaves of Dutch paper and bound in yellow morocco, the Address was as fancy as a valentine, decorated with Her Majesty's coat of arms, a British ship plunging through waves, and the towers of Windsor Castle.

For his fellow clubmen, however, the joys of a royal charter were soon mitigated. Highhandedly, Whistler abolished their old style of hanging pictures. They had in the past jammed as many as possible on the walls; Whistler insisted that works be given adequate surrounding space. This meant that far fewer painters could be represented at the club's periodic exhibits, and those left out were inevitably the older men whose styles Whistler disliked. The sale of their works, in consequence, dropped sharply. Worse, while the old members were being neglected, the upstart president invited Claude Monet, a *Frenchman*, to be a guest exhibitor. In 1888, under pressure, Whistler resigned from the presidency and the Society, after which 25 young members, including Walter Sickert, turned in their resignations in protest. Whistler commented: "The Artists came out and the British remained."

The quip was in character, but it lacked the scorpion sting of most of Whistler's witticisms—and that was perhaps a reflection of the fact that he was beginning to enjoy the greatest happiness he had ever known. It came, at almost the same moment that he was being forced out of the Royal Society of British Artists, in the form of a young art student named Beatrix Godwin, daughter of the sculptor John Birnie Philip, and wife of Whistler's old friend Edward Godwin, who had been the architect of the ill-fated White House. Trixie, as Whistler called her, was some 20 years younger than he and some 40 pounds overweight; she was, however, pretty as well as plump. She had studied art in Paris, and mixed freely in bohemian circles. She idolized Whistler. Even before the death of her husband in 1886, Trixie spent so much time in Whistler's studio that Maud Franklin protested bitterly.

Not long before he and Trixie married, Whistler did a portrait called *Harmony in Red: Lamplight* that showed his young admirer radiating warmth against a red background and wearing a red cape that tact-

During his two-year term—from 1886 to 1888—as president of the Society of British Artists, Whistler made several important innovations in the techniques of exhibiting art. The contemporary sketch above shows the Society's gallery with a fabric velarium, or canopy, that Whistler ordered hung to diffuse the overhead light; he also revolutionized the method of displaying works, insisting that they not be crowded high upon the walls but carefully spaced out. His ideas are in common use today.

fully hid her weight. With her hands on her hips, and her smiling face slightly tilted, Trixie looked as if she could good-naturedly manage anything in the world, including James Whistler. Initially both Trixie and Whistler appeared somewhat allergic to marriage. ("I don't marry," Whistler once said, "though I tolerate those who do.") Not the least of the obstacles was Maud Franklin, who was no easy loser. There was no guarantee, if the wedding should take place, that Maud might not come charging into the church to break it up.

Somewhat underhandedly, Whistler solved that problem. He wrote to a friend and disciple, an artist named William Stott, that Maud was "unwell," and suggested that Stott and his wife invite "Madame" to spend a few days with them in the country. Maud went, and learned of Whistler's marriage to Trixie on August 11, 1888, when Stott read the wedding notice aloud to her from *The Times*. (Maud missed the account in *The Pall Mall Gazette*, whose headline read: THE BUTTERFLY CHAINED AT LAST.) She called herself "Mrs. Whistler" until she married a South American—whose name is unknown—and moved off to South America with her husband and Whistler's daughter. Before Whistler's marriage Maud had been painted by Stott as a nude Venus. The naked Maud, exhibited in 1887 at the Society of British Artists, was recognizably the same girl portrayed in bonnet and furs in the same show in a painting *(page 137)* by Whistler—a coincidence that caused much gossiping among the older members of the Society.

Trixie had a tranquilizing effect on Whistler. Unlike his mistresses, who had not been welcome among all his friends, she could dine anywhere with him, and her presence in company tended to make him less combative. She held a far more prominent position in his life than any other woman ever had. He liked to have her in his studio at their new home on Tite Street in Chelsea. Once when she saw him painting brown eyes on a blue-eyed sitter—brown being better suited to his color arrangement—Trixie grabbed a brush and began changing the eyes to blue. In horror, Whistler cried, "Don't, Trixie, don't." But Trixie did. And he let her get away with it.

Trixie did not, however, entirely tame her monster. In fact, in one of the major uproars of his last years, she helped spur him into combat. The affair began when a young U.S. journalist, Sheridan Ford, asked permission to collect a batch of reviews hostile to Whistler, along with the artist's own fiery replies to the press, and publish them in a book. Whistler gave approval. But after Ford had been working for several months, Whistler decided, at Trixie's suggestion, that it was foolish to let Ford collect all the profits. He sent Ford £10 for his work to date and withdrew his permission altogether. In angry defiance, Ford went ahead and had the book printed illegally in Antwerp.

In the ensuing hullabaloo of telegrams, threats and lawsuits, Ford and his project were just about liquidated. In 1890 Whistler's own version of the book came out, under Ford's clever title, *The Gentle Art of Making Enemies*; it was in this book that Whistler rewrote the testimony at the Ruskin trial. Although it was a highly original compendium of critical stupidity, the book had little success.

In any case, all the publicity connected with *The Gentle Art* added to Whistler's expanding reputation. His work was shown in Amsterdam and Munich, and he was elected an honorary member of the Bavarian Royal Academy. He was also again causing a stir in France. In the great International Exposition of 1887 no fewer than 50 of his small oils, along with other works, were included with paintings by such important artists as Monet, Renoir, Pissarro and Sisley. Whistler was avidly discussed. Pissarro, for example, was struck by his "quite superior etchings," and surprised that they seemed so luminous, "which is strange for an artist who does not aim for this in his color." With his painter's intuition, Pissarro had sensed in the etchings a paradox that has puzzled others: they often seem more colored than Whistler's paintings themselves.

But most surprising, although consistent with his more relaxed way of life, was Whistler's growing interest in the small oils. These, in contrast to the portraits on which he had expended so much labor in his earlier years, he seemed to paint spontaneously and joyously. Usually he chose unpretentious subjects: Chelsea shopfronts, farmyards, quiet beaches, street peddlers, children playing—the poetry of the familiar.

He did not, of course, abandon portraiture. In 1891 he executed a study of young Count Robert de Montesquiou, a rich Parisian esthete who lived in a perfumed eyrie atop his father's mansion and sometimes carried a gilded tortoise. Whistler caught the self-importance of this bizarre fop and managed to suggest his peculiarities with no trace of condescension.

Good things continued to befall the artist. The French government made him an Officer of the Legion of Honor—he loved wearing the red rosette—and pleased him even more by purchasing in 1891, under pressure from admirers, including the formidable politician Georges Clemenceau, Whistler's *Mother*. In crowing over the honor, a London newspaper forgot Whistler's nationality: "Modern British art will now be represented in the National Gallery of the Luxembourg by one of the finest paintings due to the brush of an English artist."

An index to Whistler's more relaxed state of mind was his behavior toward a deputation from the city of Glasgow that visited him in 1891 to discuss buying his portrait of Thomas Carlyle, which Whistler had somehow acquired before the old Scot's death in 1881. Whistler's price was 1,000 guineas. A spokesman asked whether that was not too high, considering that the figure of Carlyle was not life size. Smilingly, Whistler replied, "But, you know, few men are life size."

With Scottish firmness, they offered £800. With charm, Whistler refused. "Now think it over, Mr. Whistler," they advised, "and we will be coming back again." When they returned the next day, Whistler was more gracious than ever; he could afford the luxury of keeping them dangling. "Have you thought of the thousand guineas," they asked, "and what we said about it, Mr. Whistler?" "Why, gentlemen," was the reply, "how could I think of anything but the pleasure of seeing you again?" They gave up, and paid the 1,000 guineas.

He also began to attract increasing recognition from his homeland.

La Princesse du Pays de la Porcelaine was taken down from her niche in the Peacock Room and shown at a Chicago exhibit in 1893—loaned by Leyland, of all people. At the same time, Whistler was asked to do a mural for the new Boston Public Library. He planned a lordly 10-foot peacock to strut over a stairway. But in his new mood he had little sense of urgency, and never got around to painting it. Now so many Americans were trying to get him to execute work that he joked, "They want to pour California into my lap."

Free of financial worries, Whistler and Trixie in 1892 decided to move permanently to Paris. Paris had run through Whistler's life like a recurring musical theme, and now it seemed an auspicious time for the theme to be repeated. Paris appreciated him. And his success at the Goupil gallery, which staged a well-received retrospective exhibit of his work that same year, testified that he was quitting London not in defeat, but on the crest of approval.

The Whistlers were lucky to find a secluded apartment at 110 Rue du Bac. The entrance was in a courtyard, reached by a long passageway from the street. Inside, the 17th Century drawing room opened, through French doors, into a large, wooded, private park, adjacent to a monastery whose chanting monks added to the other-world atmosphere. For work, he rented a top-floor studio several blocks away, reached by six flights of stairs. It rewarded him with a spectacular view across the lawns of the Luxembourg Palace and museum.

When he was home with Trixie, he enjoyed having people drop in and overflow into the garden. Calling on the celebrated Mr. Whistler became a must, like visiting the new Eiffel Tower. William Dean Howells came by with his son and daughter, of whom Whistler made a lithograph. So did the popular new painter and fellow American, John Singer Sargent, who was always deferential to the older artist. For Whistler, it was a little like being canonized before he died.

Perhaps the most striking young talent Whistler met in Paris was Aubrey Beardsley aged 21. At first Whistler was put off by his "aestheticism and decadence." Nevertheless, he invited Beardsley to one of his festive Sunday breakfasts. Later, when the young man showed him his India-ink drawings for a new edition of Alexander Pope's 18th Century poem "The Rape of the Lock," Whistler studied them and finally spoke: "Aubrey, I have made a very great mistake . . . you are a very great artist." Overwhelmed, Beardsley broke into tears.

Lest it appear that in his happy role as grand old man of art Whistler was sinking into maudlin benevolence, it must be reported that he got into a frightful row with Sir William Eden about the payment for a portrait of Lady Eden. Eden had ordered a small study of his wife at a price of 100 to 150 guineas; Whistler executed a life-sized painting, for which his charge would of course have been far more. Eden paid only 100 guineas. Whistler kept the portrait and Eden sued. Whistler had four years of excitement with the case, dragging it in and out of two courts before he was ordered to return Eden's 100 guineas and alter the portrait so that it no longer resembled Lady Eden.

Another ruckus ensued when Whistler discovered that his old friend

George du Maurier had written nastily about him in *Trilby*, an immensely popular novel about their student days in Paris that was being serialized in the U.S. magazine *Harper's*. In words and drawings Whistler was recognizably depicted as a charming but cowardly cad. Whistler demanded and obtained an apology from *Harper's*, and when the novel was published in book form du Maurier altered the character so that he no longer resembled Whistler.

For all such occasional perturbations, Whistler's stay in Paris was idyllic; Trixie had spells of ill health, but he attached no significance to them. A source of comfort and inspiration was his friendship with the symbolist poet Stéphane Mallarmé. The relationship illumines the final development of Whistler's art. Just as 40 years earlier he had been fortified by Courbet's earthy realism, so now he was in tune with another potent, although opposing, current of French thought.

To liken poetry to painting can be misleading. But it is fair to say that Mallarmé's approach to poetry was markedly similar to Whistler's approach to art. Both men felt that certain experiences could best be expressed by nuance and implication. They both tried to capture that "sacred something else"—Mallarmé by the music of language and symbolic images, Whistler by his subtle blending of tones and arrangements of form. This was not meant as an evasion of literal truth, but as a way of reaching deeper, hidden truths.

This was the prevailing mood in French art. It was being expressed musically by Claude Debussy in his orchestral reverie *The Afternoon of a Faun,* which was directly inspired by Mallarmé's poem of the same name. And Debussy, again, showed his affinity to Whistler in musical tone poems that he entitled *Nocturnes* and *Fireworks*. In the fellowship of the arts, many Frenchmen now began to regard Whistler as a kindred force.

Under the combined influence of symbolist tenets and his adored Trixie, Whistler developed a stronger interest in lithography. Trixie loved to practice it herself, and her husband produced a number of lithographic works in Paris, including hazy glimpses of the Luxembourg Gardens, street scenes and people chatting, all of them intimate, informal subjects with a touch of crepuscular poignance, as if the sweetness of life were all too brief. It would be wholly unwarranted, however, to assume that Whistler's preoccupation with smaller, more evocative works signified a decline into triviality. Rather, his interest bespoke a general tendency in France among poets, and among young painters like Pierre Bonnard and Édouard Vuillard, to create small works and fleeting impressions, as if their purpose were to seize only a few rare tail feathers as the bird of truth flew by.

Considering how long Whistler had waited for the pleasures of settled domesticity, it is understandable that he refused to recognize omens of disaster. Trixie's bouts of illness became increasingly frequent. While Whistler was always solicitous, he could not face the possibility that her life was in danger. When he was finally told that Trixie was suffering from cancer, he was angrily incredulous. In a frantic attempt to make her well, he spent two years taking her from doctor to

Plump Beatrix Godwin Whistler was the target of *The Fat Woman*, a caricature drawn by Aubrey Beardsley in the 1890s. Many of the artist's friends disliked the bride Whistler took when he was 54, and their feeling was fueled by sympathy for Maud Franklin, Whistler's mistress for a decade; at times, Beatrix was referred to as "the fat thing."

173

In 1903 a group of Whistler admirers asked sculptor Auguste Rodin to execute a "Winged Victory" as a memorial to the artist. The choice of subject was surprising in light of Whistler's disdain for allegorical works; even more surprising was Rodin's acceptance, for he too had turned from the classical mode. Inevitably, the project was a fiasco. Rodin tarried five years before unveiling to a shocked committee the model for an armless Venus *(above)*. It was rejected. He then added arms, a lantern and a disk inscribed with Whistler's face *(below)*; it too was rejected.

doctor. He fought with his brother, Dr. William Whistler, for warning him that Trixie might be fatally ill, and he put her case in the hands of an obscure French doctor who planned to operate. Dr. Whistler rushed over to Paris just in time to halt the operation, which he said could do no good and would cause Trixie unnecessary torment. After a savage quarrel, Whistler foreswore his brother's friendship.

Still hopeful, Whistler installed his wife in a bedroom at London's new Hotel Savoy, with a lovely view of the Thames. He frequently sat by her bed, etching and making lithographs, and produced one touching portrait of Trixie leaning against a mountain of pillows. Refusing to imply that she was in bed for any serious reason, he named it *By the Balcony (page 166)*. As her condition worsened, he took her to a nursing home on Hampstead Heath. Trixie died of cancer on May 10, 1896. At the hour of her death a friend saw Whistler running across the heath, demented with grief. "Don't speak! Don't speak! It is terrible," he cried, and stumbled onward. He would never admit the cause of her death, and refused even to notify his brother that she had died.

From then on, it seemed, Whistler never stopped running. He traveled abroad, to Algiers, Corsica and Morocco. He moved to several different London hotels and sometimes stayed with friends. But none of his old friends were left. He had somehow alienated the great confidant of his youth, Fantin-Latour, who in later years would say of Whistler that he had "little respect" for his character. Rossetti and Mallarmé had died. Occasionally, he saw his half sister, Deborah, but of course not in the company of her husband, Dr. Seymour Haden, with whom he had broken so many years before. And he had quarreled, sometimes cruelly, with such young disciples as Walter Sickert, Mortimer Menpes, and the worshipful Greaves brothers who used to row his boats on the Thames.

In his last years Whistler was comforted by a contingent of young Americans, some of them very rich, who appeared like a band of guardian angels to buy his paintings and honor his achievements. A young couple from Pennsylvania, the Joseph Pennells, became his official biographers, and with Boswellian fervor produced two huge works on the artist, a *Life* and a *Journal*. And two multimillionaires, Henry Frick and Charles Freer, gathered important collections of his works.

In these final restless years Whistler could not complain that he was being ignored, professionally or socially. Several major exhibits of his work were held, and when he fell ill in 1902 in Holland, the Queen of the Netherlands was sufficiently impressed by her artistic visitor to send him the court physician. But if Whistler could assess his importance today, he might have cause both for complaint and some unexpected satisfactions.

His Art for Art's Sake crusade, although an important corrective to popular Victorian art, is not permanently valid; it is a delusion, of course, that art is ever pure or independent. The esteem in which his painting is held today is often grudging because, amid the explosive colors and patterns of most modern painting, Whistler's low-key arrangements sometimes appear tame. Yet ultimately he triumphs exactly as he wished. His intense devotion to his craft and his poetic sensibilities have produced a small but highly distinguished body of art. Beauty wins out. In half a dozen portraits, in his Nocturnes and etchings, there is a strength that deserves to be called magical.

Whistler's influence on English art was incalculable. He broke the fusty spell of the Academy. He taught other artists not how to paint but how to *look*—selectively. He took them to school to the Orient. And he imbued them with his ideal of abstract art, art existing for itself alone. Whistler's ideal was not the whole truth, but there could be no truth without it.

It is tempting to say that Whistler as an artist was more important than his art. Certainly the man himself was more spectacular, more exasperating, more sympathetic than anything he ever created. To Henry Adams, writing in his *Education*, Whistler was a "witty, declamatory, extravagant, bitter, amusing, noisy" man who nevertheless spoke the truth and showed "a willingness to seem eccentric where no real eccentricity, unless perhaps of temper, existed." Henry James, similarly, saw behind the man and his art, and realized that such tireless dedication to perfection must be a source of anguish. "You have done too much of the exquisite," James wrote to Whistler, "not to have earned more despair, than anything else."

In his final illness, probably chronic influenza, Whistler had little energy left to keep his public image polished. He had moved into his fourth home on the Chelsea embankment, nursed by his wife's sister and her mother. Like an old lion trying to roar, he threatened to sue his next-door neighbors for hammering too loudly as they made household repairs, but no suit was filed. Too ill to play the dandy, he shuffled around the house in an old fur coat. With visitors he played dominoes, cheating a bit. He had his bedroom moved downstairs next to his studio, so that he could paint whenever he had strength, and he hired a full-lipped Irish model, Dorothy Seton, who had flowing red hair like Jo's and Maud's. His tender portrait of Dorothy holding an apple, called *Daughter of Eve*, was the finest work of his last period. "How long do you think it took me to paint that?" he asked Joseph Pennell. Beaming with triumph, Whistler answered himself: "A couple of hours, *this very morning!*" For once, the artist had not been tempted to repaint or rub out, as if now that he was casting off his mortal form he was also casting off his doubts and inhibitions.

The end came in his Chelsea home on July 17, 1903. The funeral was held in Old Chelsea Church. The last rites took place in a cemetery at nearby Chiswick where he was interred beside his wife.

Whistler had died so suddenly that the doctor was unable to reach his deathbed. Certainly, of all men, Whistler would have liked to confront death with an irreverent quip. But there is no report that he spoke a single word of farewell. His attitude toward dying, however, is on record in a typical little joke he tossed off in Paris, when friends complained of climbing the six flights to see him in his studio. Why in the world, they panted, didn't he have a studio on the ground floor?

"When I die," he said, laughing, "I will."

After his death Whistler, who had been a lifelong cigarette smoker, was given the questionable distinction of having a cigar named after him. The lithograph above, which presents a clumsy array of the artist's works while misspelling his middle names—"Abbott" and "McNeill"—graced boxes of cigars rolled by Leopold Powell and Company of Tampa, Florida. Whistler, via advertisements, was also made out to be a posthumous advocate for a New York clothing store, a line of stationary and, perhaps most incongruously, the Pierce-Arrow automobile.

175

One day in Paris in November 1894 Whistler's servant announced that a gentleman named Charles Lang Freer was waiting to see him. When the artist went downstairs he found a diminutive, impeccably groomed youngish man who said, "I'm an American, Mr. Whistler, just from America. I heard that you made an etching once and I would like to see it." Whistler surveyed him for a moment, then took him into the studio. Freer later admitted that he had intentionally made himself out to be an innocent provincial abroad; apparently Whistler enjoyed impressing him, for he offered an invitation to lunch. Soon the two became fast friends.

A Detroit multimillionaire who had made his fortune in railroads, Freer had actually been collecting Whistler etchings and pastels for several years. After meeting the artist he started buying Whistlers in earnest, from the painter himself or from owners willing to sell. His collection became the largest in the world.

When Freer met Whistler the artist had only nine more years to live—and when he died in 1903 an unfinished portrait of Freer (opposite) was on his easel. Those last years—indeed, the last two decades of his life —remained productive ones for Whistler. His paintings of this period included several magnificent portraits and many small works, mostly townscapes and seascapes distinguished by their delicacy and lack of pretension. To the end, his was an art of understatement.

A Patron's Taste

Whistler did not live to complete this portrait of his friend and patron Charles Freer, but even in its unfinished state it shows the intensity of an indefatigable collector. Freer shared with Whistler a love of Far Eastern art and often traveled great distances to search out objects of rare beauty. He was equally zealous in his pursuit of Whistler paintings; among those he brought to the U.S. were many of the works shown on the following pages.

Portrait of Charles Lang Freer, c. 1902

Two of Whistler's finest late portraits recall earlier ones. Like the portraits of Mr. and Mrs. Frederick Leyland *(pages 116 and 117)*, the two shown here present the lady in a froth of rosy hues and the gentleman in austere black. Whistler's portrayal of Mrs. Leyland, however, was a study in soft elegance. This painting, of the wife of a wealthy brewer, Lady Meux, shows a full-blown beauty with a ripe figure and imperious air. Even the colors, although in the same range, seem more intense, hotter. Where once Whistler customarily showed young women as ethereal, virginal types, this work reveals an appreciation of substance, of the here and now.

By comparison with Whistler's painting of Frederick Leyland, the portrait on the opposite page, of the French art critic Théodore Duret, shows a considerable deepening of character revelation. Noted not only for his good looks but also for his courageous support of young artists, Duret was an admirer of Whistler's and the feeling was mutual. While the Frenchman was in London on a business trip, Whistler asked him to pose in evening dress, recalling the challenge he had set himself in the portrait of Leyland. But this time Whistler accented the black of the suit with the subtle pinkish-gray lining of Duret's cape, called a domino, and the bold red fan. The brilliant contrast adds to the impression of strength revealed in the man's sensitive face.

Valerie, Lady Meux, 1881

Arrangement in Flesh Color and Black: Portrait of Théodore Duret, 1882-1884

A Note in Red, 1880s

In the 1880s Whistler began to paint small studies of coast, country and city scenes. Like Impressionist paintings, they are efforts to capture a moment in time and he painted them as his French colleagues were painting: swiftly, and from nature. Early in the morning he would arrive in London's picturesque Chelsea district with his little box of oils, choose a subject—often a row of storefronts with passing shoppers—borrow a chair from the nearest shopkeeper and work until lunchtime, unperturbed by the swarms of children who flocked around him. *Chelsea Shops (upper right)*, its tiny figures moving in a rhythmic cadence in front of the building façades, is the result of such a session.

Sometimes he would select a more tranquil spot for a cityscape, like *A Note in Red (above)*, in which the symmetrically aligned houses are viewed from across a wide road and a broad green, and the pattern of receding planes gives an impression of peaceful expanse, in spite of the picture's small size —it is less than 10 inches wide.

In *Grey and Silver (right)*, Whistler returned to one of his favorite subjects, the sea, capturing it in a sullen mood: the cold green water roiled with waves, the sky chilled and foreboding.

THE SMITHSONIAN INSTITUTION, FREER GALLERY OF ART, WASHINGTON, D.C.

Chelsea Shops, 1880s

THE SMITHSONIAN INSTITUTION, FREER GALLERY OF ART, WASHINGTON, D.C.

Grey and Silver: The Angry Sea, early 1880s

A "sketch of skys and tops of houses," in Whistler's words, this canvas was painted at Lyme Regis, a resort on the Dorset coast of England where he had taken his wife for the summer. Just over two feet wide, it is the largest landscape he ever executed.

The simple, bucolic scene is painted in broadly brushed, harmonizing tones of the browns, grays and greens he loved. Its gentle mood is a reminder of the qualities in Whistler's art that appealed to Freer: reticence and refinement. Painter and patron alike

Dorsetshire Landscape, 1895

worshiped the serenity of Oriental art with its stylized simplification of nature, and the economy of treatment that Whistler used to convey the peaceful ambience of this village shows the influence of his study of Eastern technique.

After the deaths of his wife and family left Whistler bereft of his old circle, his friendship with the bachelor Freer deepened: the last engagement he had was for a carriage drive with Freer. He died while Freer was on the way to call for him.

183

Self-Portrait, c. 1900

To Whistler, American

On the loan exhibit of his paintings at the Tate Gallery.

You also, our first great,
Had tried all ways;
Tested and pried and worked in many fashions,
And this much gives me heart to play the game.

Here is a part that's slight, and part gone wrong,
And much of little moment, and some few
Perfect as Dürer!
"In the Studio" and these two portraits, if I had my
　　choice!
And then these sketches in the mood of Greece?

You had your searches, your uncertainties,
And this is good to know—for us, I mean,
Who bear the brunt of our America
And try to wrench her impulse into art.

You were not always sure, not always set
To hiding night or tuning "symphonies";
Had not one style from birth, but tried and pried
And stretched and tampered with the media.

You and Abe Lincoln from that mass of dolts
Show us there's chance at least of winning through.

—Ezra Pound

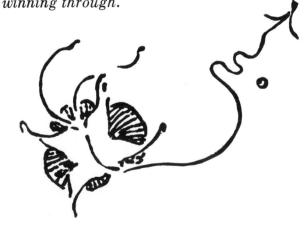

First published in "Poetry" magazine, 1912. Ezra Pound,
"Personae." Copyright 1926 by Ezra Pound. Reprinted
by permission of New Directions Publishing Corporation.

Chronology: Artists of Whistler's Era

1700	1825	1950

UNITED STATES
THOMAS COLE   1801-1848
WILLIAM SIDNEY MOUNT   1807-1868
GEORGE CALEB BINGHAM   1811-1879
ALBERT BIERSTADT   1830-1902
JAMES ABBOTT McNEILL WHISTLER   1834-1903
WINSLOW HOMER   1836-1910
THOMAS EAKINS   1844-1916
MARY CASSATT   1845-1926
FRANK DUVENECK   1848-1919
WILLIAM M. CHASE   1849-1916
OTTO BACHER   1856-1909
JOHN SINGER SARGENT   1856-1925
JOSEPH PENNELL   1860-1926

FRANCE
JEAN-AUGUSTE-DOMINIQUE INGRES   1780-1867
THÉODORE GÉRICAULT   1791-1824
EUGÉNE DELACROIX   1798-1863
HORACE LECOCQ DE BOISBAUDRAN   1802-1897
CHARLES GLEYRE (Swiss)   1808-1874
CHARLES-FRANÇOIS DAUBIGNY   1817-1878
GUSTAVE COURBET   1819-1877
AUGUSTE DELÂTRE   1822-1907
CAMILLE PISSARRO   1831-1903
ÉDOUARD MANET   1832-1883
FÉLIX BRACQUEMOND   1833-1914
EDGAR DEGAS   1834-1917
JAMES TISSOT   1836-1902
HENRI FANTIN-LATOUR   1836-1904
ALPHONSE LEGROS   1837-1911
ALFRED SISLEY   1839-1899
PAUL CÉZANNE   1839-1906
ODILON REDON   1840-1916
AUGUSTE RODIN   1840-1917
CLAUDE MONET   1840-1926
PIERRE-AUGUSTE RENOIR   1841-1919
PAUL GAUGUIN   1848-1903
GEORGES SEURAT   1859-1891
PIERRE BONNARD   1867-1947
ÉDOUARD VUILLARD   1868-1940

JAPAN
TORII KIYONAGA   1742-1815
HOKUSAI   1760-1849
HIROSHIGE I   1797-1858

ENGLAND
WILLIAM HOGARTH   1697-1764
SIR JOSHUA REYNOLDS   1723-1792
WILLIAM BLAKE   1757-1827
J. M. W. TURNER   1775-1851
JOHN CONSTABLE   1776-1837
SIR WILLIAM ALLEN (Scottish)   1782-1850
SIR WILLIAM BOXALL   1800-1879
SIR EDWIN LANDSEER   1802-1873
AUGUSTUS EGG   1816-1863
ALFRED STEVENS   1817-1875
GEORGE FREDERIC WATTS   1817-1904
FRANCIS SEYMOUR HADEN   1818-1910
ALFRED RANKLEY   1819-1872
WILLIAM POWELL FRITH   1819-1909
FORD MADOX BROWN   1821-1893
MRS. SOPHIE ANDERSON   1823-c. 1898
WILLIAM LINDSAY WINDUS   1823-1907
JAMES COLLINSON   c. 1825-1881
THOMAS WOOLNER   1825-1892
ROBERT BRAITHWAITE MARTINEAU   1826-1869
WALTER DEVERELL   1827-1854
WILLIAM HOLMAN HUNT   1827-1910
DANTE GABRIEL ROSSETTI   1828-1882
FREDERIC GEORGE STEPHENS   1828-1907
SIR JOHN EVERETT MILLAIS   1829-1896
WILLIAM MICHAEL ROSSETTI   1829-1919
LORD FREDERIC LEIGHTON   1830-1896
HENRY MOORE   1831-1896
ARTHUR HUGHES   1832-1915
SIR EDWARD BURNE-JONES   1833-1898
PHILIP HERMOGENES CALDERON   1833-1898
GEORGE HENRY BOUGHTON   1833-1905
WILLIAM MORRIS   1834-1896
LAWRENCE ALMA-TADEMA   1836-1912
SIR JOHN EDWARD POYNTER   1836-1919
VALENTINE PRINSEP   1838-1904
ALBERT JOSEPH MOORE   1841-1893
SIR LUKE FILDES   1844-1927
WALTER GREAVES   1846-1930
MORTIMER MENPES (Australian)   1859-1938
WALTER SICKERT   1860-1942
AUBREY BEARDSLEY   1872-1898
SIR MAX BEERBOHM   1872-1956

1700	1825	1950

Whistler's predecessors, contemporaries and successors are grouped here in chronological order according to country. The bands correspond to the life spans of the artists.

Bibliography

*Available in paperback

WHISTLER—HIS LIFE AND WORK

Bacher, Otto H., *With Whistler in Venice*. The Century Co., 1908.
Gallatin, A. E., *Portraits of Whistler, A Critical Study and an Iconography*. John Lane Co., 1918.
Laver, James, *Whistler*. Faber and Faber, London, 1930.
Parry, Albert, *Whistler's Father*. The Bobbs-Merrill Co., 1939.
Pearson, Hesketh, *The Man Whistler*. Harper & Bros., 1952.
Pennell, Elizabeth Robins and Joseph:
    The Life of James McNeill Whistler, 6th rev. ed. J. B. Lippincott Co., 1919.
    The Whistler Journal. J. B. Lippincott Co., 1921.
Sutton, Denys:
    James McNeill Whistler: Paintings, Etchings, Pastels & Watercolors. Phaidon Press, London, 1966.
    Nocturne: The Art of James McNeill Whistler. J. B. Lippincott Co., 1964.
Whistler, J. A. M., *The Gentle Art of Making Enemies*.* Introduction by Alfred Werner. Dover Publications, Inc., 1967.

ART-HISTORICAL BACKGROUND

Bell, Quentin, *Victorian Artists*. Harvard University Press, 1967.
Doughty, Oswald, *Dante Gabriel Rossetti, A Victorian Romantic*. Yale University Press, 1949.
The Early Work of Aubrey Beardsley, reprint ed. Da Capo Press, 1967.
Fleming, G. H., *Rossetti and the Pre-Raphaelite Brotherhood*. Rupert Hart-Davis, London, 1967.
Fredeman, William E., *Pre-Raphaelitism, A Bibliocritical Study*. Harvard University Press, 1965.
Gaunt, William, *The Pre-Raphaelite Dream*.* Schocken Books, 1966.
Hind, Arthur M., *A History of Engraving and Etching from the 15th Century to the Year 1914*,* 3rd rev. ed. Dover Publications, Inc., 1963.
Ironside, R., and J. A. Gere, *Pre-Raphaelite Painters*. Phaidon Press, London, 1948.
James, Henry, *The Painter's Eye: Notes and Essays on the Pictorial Arts*. Introduction by John L. Sweeney. Harvard University Press. 1956.
The Later Work of Aubrey Beardsley, reprint ed. Da Capo Press, 1967.
Leon, Derrick, *Ruskin, The Great Victorian*. Routledge & Kegan Paul, London, 1949.
Lister, Raymond, *Victorian Narrative Paintings*. Clarkson N. Potter, Inc., 1966.
Lumsden, E. S., *The Art of Etching*. Dover Publications, Inc., 1962.
Maas, Jeremy, *Victorian Painters*. Barrie and Rockliff, The Cresset Press, London, 1969.
Ormond, Leonée, *George du Maurier*. Routledge & Kegan Paul, London, 1969.

Reynolds, Graham, *Victorian Painting*. The Macmillan Company, 1967.
Rosenberg, John D., *The Darkening Glass, A Portrait of Ruskin's Genius*. Columbia University Press, 1961.

CULTURAL AND HISTORICAL BACKGROUND

Ambrose, Stephen E., *Duty, Honor, Country—A History of West Point*. The Johns Hopkins Press, 1966.
Ames, Winslow, *Prince Albert and Victorian Taste*. The Viking Press, 1968.
Grebanier, Frances Winwar, *Poor Splendid Wings: The Rossettis and Their Circle*. Little, Brown & Co., 1933.
Harris, Frank, *Oscar Wilde, His Life & Confessions*. Covici-Friede Publishers, 1930.
Henderson, Philip, *William Morris, His Life, Work and Friends*. Thames and Hudson, London, 1967.
Lutyens, Mary, *Millais and the Ruskins*. Vanguard Press, Inc., 1968.
Manvell, Roger, *Ellen Terry*. G. P. Putnam's Sons, 1968.
Miller, Perry, *The Life of the Mind in America from the Revolution to the Civil War*. Harcourt, Brace & World, Inc., 1965.
Queen Victoria, *Leaves from a Journal, 1855*. Introduction by Raymond Mortimer. Farrar, Straus & Cudahy, 1961.
Terry, Ellen, *The Story of My Life*. Hutchinson & Co., London, 1908.
Thompson, Paul, *The Work of William Morris*. The Viking Press, 1967.

EXHIBITION CATALOGUES

James McNeill Whistler, An Exhibition of Paintings and Other Works. The Arts Council Gallery, London, and The Knoedler Galleries, 1960.
Stubbs, Burns A., *Paintings, Pastels, Drawings, Prints and Copper Plates by and Attributed to American and European Artists, Together with a List of Original Whistleriana*. Freer Gallery of Art, 1948.
Sweet, Frederick A., *James McNeill Whistler*. The Art Institute of Chicago, 1968.

PERIODICALS

De Caso, Jacques, "1861: Hokusai rue Jacob." *The Burlington Magazine*, Vol. CXI (Sept. 1969), pp. 562 and 565.
Sandberg, John, "'Japonisme' and Whistler." *The Burlington Magazine*, Vol. CVI (Nov. 1964), pp. 500-507.
Staley, Allen, "The Condition of Music." *Art News Annual*, Vol. 33 (1966-1967), pp. 81-87.
Storrow, Thomas, "George Washington Whistler in Stonington." *Bulletin of the Stonington Historical Society*, Vol. III (May 1966).

Picture credits

The sources for the illustrations in this book appear below. Credits for pictures from left to right are separated by semicolons, from top to bottom by dashes.

SLIPCASE: Tate Gallery, London.

FRONT END PAPERS: Courtesy of the Smithsonian Institution, Freer Gallery of Art, Washington, D.C.

BACK END PAPERS: Prints Division, The New York Public Library.

CHAPTER 1: 6—Prints Division, The New York Public Library. 7 —From *George du Maurier* by Leonée Ormond. Published by Routledge & Kegan Paul, London, and © University of Pittsburgh Press (1969); Prints Division, The New York Public Library. 8 —© Birmingham Museum and Art Gallery; Prints Division, The New York Public Library. 9—Prints Division, The New York Public Library; Derek Bayes. 10—Prints Division, The New York Public Library. 12—Courtesy Arthur H. Frazier. 13— Pennell Collection, Library of Congress, Washington, D.C.— Courtesy of the Smithsonian Institution, Freer Gallery of Art, Washington, D.C. 14—Pennell Collection, Library of Congress, Washington, D.C. 15—Library of Congress, Washington, D.C. 16—Pennell Collection, Library of Congress, Washington, D.C. 18—United States Military Academy Archives and History Office, West Point. 19—Courtesy The Art Institute of Chicago. 21— Pennell Collection, Library of Congress, Washington, D.C. 24— *Harper's Monthly Magazine* (1894). 27—Photo des Musées Nationaux. 28—Prints Division, The New York Public Library. 29—Courtesy of the Smithsonian Institution, Freer Gallery of Art, Washington, D.C. 30, 31—Carlo Bavagnoli; The Taft Museum, Cincinnati, Ohio—City Art Museum of Saint Louis. 32—Courtesy of the Smithsonian Institution, Freer Gallery of Art, Washington, D.C. 33—Giraudon—Frank Lerner. 34, 35—From the Collection of Mr. and Mrs. John Hay Whitney.

CHAPTER 2: 36—Heinz Zinram. 40—Pennell Collection, Library of Congress, Washington, D.C.—From *The Whistler Journal* by E. R. & J. Pennell (1921). 42—Cincinnati Art Museum. 43— Derek Bayes from *The Life of Whistler* by E. R. & J. Pennell (1908). 44—Punch Publications Ltd., London. 49, 50, 51— Tate Gallery, London. 52, 53—Derek Bayes. 54—Pierre Boulat. 55—Derek Bayes. 56, 57—Dr. René Taylor courtesy Ponce Art Museum; Robert Ragsdale. 58, 59—Heinz Zinram.

CHAPTER 3: 60—National Gallery of Art, Washington, D.C. 62— © Birmingham Museum and Art Gallery. 64—Alan Clifton— William Morris Gallery, Walthamstow. 65—William Morris Gallery, Walthamstow. 66—© Radio Times Hulton Picture Library. 67—Pennell Collection, Library of Congress, Washington, D.C. 69—Derek Bayes. 70, 71—Tate Gallery, London except top left Derek Bayes. 72—Herbert Orth. 73—Courtesy The Wadsworth Atheneum, Hartford, Connecticut. 74, 75—Manchester City Art Galleries.

CHAPTER 4: 76—Courtesy of the Smithsonian Institution, Freer Gallery of Art, Washington, D.C. 78—Historical Pictures Service, Chicago. 81—Victoria and Albert Museum, London except left Munson-Williams-Proctor Institute. 82—Pennell Collection, Library of Congress, Washington, D.C. 86—Historical Pictures Service, Chicago. 89, 90, 91—Staatliche Museen, Berlin, courtesy Tate Gallery, London. 92, 93—Courtesy of the Smithsonian Institution, Freer Gallery of Art, Washington, D.C.; A. J. Wyatt courtesy John G. Johnson Collection, Philadelphia. 94—By courtesy of the Trustees of the British Museum, London; Courtesy Museum of Fine Arts, Boston—Courtesy of the Smithsonian Institution, Freer Gallery of Art, Washington, D.C. 95—Courtesy The Art Institute of Chicago. 96, 97—Courtesy of the Smithsonian Institution, Freer Gallery of Art, Washington, D.C.; Derek Bayes. 98, 99—Derek Bayes.

CHAPTER 5: 100—Courtesy of the Smithsonian Institution, Freer Gallery of Art, Washington, D.C. 104, 105—Pennell Collection, Library of Congress, Washington, D.C. 108—Derek Bayes. 113 —Derek Bayes. 114—Photo des Musées Nationaux. 115—Glasgow Art Gallery and Museum. 116—Courtesy of the Smithsonian Institution, Freer Gallery of Art, Washington, D.C. 117—© The Frick Collection, New York. 118, 119—Courtesy of the Smithsonian Institution, Freer Gallery of Art, Washington, D.C.

CHAPTER 6: 120—The Detroit Institute of Arts. 122—Pennell Collection, Library of Congress, Washington, D.C. 128—Prints Division, The New York Public Library. 129—Pennell Collection, Library of Congress, Washington, D.C.—Prints Division, The New York Public Library. 130, 131—Pennell Collection, Library of Congress, Washington, D.C. 133, 134—The Detroit Institute of Arts. 135—Tate Gallery, London. 136, 137—Frank Lerner. 138, 139—Derek Bayes.

CHAPTER 7: 140—Fogg Art Museum courtesy Harvard University. 142—Prints Division, The New York Public Library. 146—The Philip H. & A. S. W. Rosenbach Foundation. 148—Punch Publications Ltd., London. 149—© by courtesy of the Trustees of the British Museum, London. 151 through 157—Prints Division, The New York Public Library. 158, 159—Courtesy of the Smithsonian Institution, Freer Gallery of Art, Washington, D.C. 161—Prints Division, The New York Public Library. 162 through 165—Courtesy of the Smithsonian Institution, Freer Gallery of Art, Washington, D.C.

CHAPTER 8: 166—Courtesy of the Smithsonian Institution, Freer Gallery of Art, Washington, D.C. 169—© reserved by the University of Oxford, Ashmolean Museum, Department of Western Art. 173—© Tate Gallery, London. 174—Pennell Collection, Library of Congress, Washington, D.C. 175—Prints Division, New York Public Library. 177—Courtesy of the Smithsonian Institution, Freer Gallery of Art, Washington, D.C. 178—© The Frick Collection, New York. 179—Walter Steinkopf. 180 through 183—Courtesy of the Smithsonian Institution, Freer Gallery of Art, Washington, D.C. 184—National Gallery of Art, Washington, D.C.

Acknowledgments

For their help in the preparation of this book, the author and editors wish to thank the following persons and institutions: Catherine Bélenger, Service des Relations Extérieures du Musée du Louvre, Paris; Harold Bloom, Yale University, New Haven; William A. Bostick, The Detroit Institute of Arts, Detroit; The British Museum, The Print Room, London; Isetta Cannavo, Venice; Edward Craig, Buckinghamshire; H. B. Crooks, Worcester Art Museum, Worcester; Beatrice Dabney, Dover; Louisa Dresser, Worcester Art Museum, Worcester; Edward H. Dwight, Munson-Williams-Proctor Institute, Utica; Arthur H. Frazier, Washington, D.C.; John A. Goodwin, Lowell Technological Institute, Lowell; Martyn Green, New York; Madame Guynet-Pechadre, Service Photographique, Musée du Louvre, Paris; Karen McWhirter, Metropolitan Museum of Art, New York; Julian Mason, Library of Congress, Washington, D.C.; Willa R. Moore, Smithsonian Institution, Freer Gallery of Art, Washington, D.C.; William W. Morrison, National Gallery of Art, Washington, D.C.; Edgar Munhall, The Frick Collection, New York; Leonée Ormond, London; Albert Parry, Department of Slavic Studies, Case Western Reserve University, Cleveland; John Powers, J. Walter Thompson, New York; Kenneth W. Rapp, United States Military Academy Library, West Point; Monsieur et Madame Georges Raymond, Paris; Betty Riegel, Museum of Fine Arts, Boston; Elizabeth Roth and Staff of Prints Division, The New York Public Library, New York; Madame Maurice Sérullaz, Musée du Louvre, Paris; Charles F. Stevens, United States Playing Card Company, Cincinnati; Thomas W. Storrow, Stonington Historical Society, Stonington; Denys Sutton, London; Barbara Sweeny, John G. Johnson Collection, Philadelphia; Tate Gallery, London; U.S. Coast and Geodetic Survey, Rockville; Gastone Ventura, Venice; The Victoria and Albert Museum, The Print Room, London; George L. Watson, Director, The Hill-Stead Museum, Farmington; The William Morris Gallery, Walthamstow.

Index

Numerals in italics indicate a picture of the subject mentioned. Unless otherwise identified, all listed art works are by Whistler. Dimensions are given in inches unless otherwise specified; height precedes width. Dimensions of etchings and dry points are to the plate mark.

Abbott, Mrs., Jo Heffernan's pseudonym, 41
Academic art, 56
Adams, Henry, 175
Albert, Prince, 48
Alexander, Cicely, 102-103, 112, *113*
Alexander, E. P., *19*
Alexander, W. C., 130
Alicia, Whistler's aunt, 16
Allen, Sir William, 16
Alley in Venice, 10¼ x 7, pastel, *140*, 144
Alma-Tadema, Sir Lawrence, 56, 85; *An Apodyterium*, *56-57*
Anderson, Sophie, *No Walk Today*, *36*
Angry Sea, The. See Grey and Silver: The Angry Sea
Annie Haden, 13¾ x 8⅜, dry point, *151*
Apodyterium, An, (Alma-Tadema), 17½ x 23¼, oil on canvas, *56-57*
Appeal to the Law, An, (Sambourne), caricature, *129*
Arrangement in Black and Brown: The Fur Jacket, 76⅜ x 36½, oil on canvas, *137*
Arrangement in Black and White No. 1: The Young American, 75⅜ x 35¾, oil on canvas, *100*, 124, 125
Arrangement in Black No. 3: Sir Henry Irving, 84¾ x 42¾, oil on canvas, *136*, 137
Arrangement in Black: Portrait of F. R. Leyland, 75⅞ x 36⅛, oil on canvas, *116*, 178
Arrangement in Flesh Color and Black: Portrait of Theodore Duret, 76⅛ x 35¾, oil on canvas, 147, *179*
Arrangement in Grey and Black No. 1: The Artist's Mother, 57¼ x 64¾, oil on canvas, 12, 86-87, *114*, 145-146, 171
Arrangement in Grey and Black No. 2: Thomas Carlyle, 67 x 56, oil on canvas, 102-103, *115*, 171
Arrangement in Grey: Self-Portrait, 29½ x 21, oil on canvas, *120*
Arrangement in White and Black, 146
Art: Estheticism in England, 147; French versus English, 62; influence on Whistler of Baudelaire's and Gautier's thoughts on, 25; nature versus, 43, 149, 167-168; new movements and theories in France, 45-46; Pre-Raphaelites' theories of, 62, 68; Ruskin on, 122; storytelling in, 45, 46; Victorian concepts and tastes, 48, 52-53, 54-55, 56, 126; Whistler's celebrated sentence on, 84-85; Whistler's thoughts on, 8, 12, 43, 125-127, 149; Wilde's theories on, 149
Art criticism: assessment of Whistler's work today, 174-175; comments on *White Girl*, *60*; remarks on, in Whistler's "Ten O'Clock" lecture, 167; Ruskin and, 122, 129, 145; Whistler-Ruskin trial and, 125-130; on Whistler's etchings of Venice, 145
Art exhibitions: Goupil Gallery, 172; Grosvenor Gallery, 111, 124-125; Salon des Refusés, 46, 47; shows of Whistler's work in European cities, 171, 172, 174; United States exhibit of Whistler's *Mother*, 145-146; of Venice etchings, 145, 146
Art for Art's Sake movement, 45, 46, 84; Estheticism and, 147; Whistler's attitude toward, 8, 12, 168, 174
Art Nouveau style, 65-66
Artist in His Studio, The, 24¾ x 18¾, oil on panel, 94, *95*
Artist's Mother, The. See Arrangement in Grey and Black No. 1
Arts Club, 121, 130
At the Piano, 26⅜ x $36\frac{1}{10}$, 25, *30 31*, 38-39, 42
Axenfeld, 8⅞ x 5⅞, dry point, *153*

Bab sketch (Gilbert), *149*
Bacher, Otto, 142-143, 144-145
Balcony, The. See Variations in Flesh Color and Green
Baleful Head, The, (Burne-Jones), 61 x 51, oil on canvas, *72*
Baudelaire, Charles, 25
Beardsley, Aubrey, works of *9*, *173*
Becquet, 10 x 7½, etching and dry point, *152*
Beerbohm, Max, caricature by, *8*
"Before the Mirror: Versus under a Picture" (Swinburne), *80*
Bellelli Family, The, (Degas), 80 x 101, oil on canvas, *30*
Benham, Captain Henry, 21, 22
Berners Street Gallery, 44
Black Lion Wharf, 5⅞ x 8⅞, etching, *156-157*; reproduced in *Mother*, *114*
Blue Wave: Biarritz, The, 24½ x 34, oil on canvas, *33*, 43
Boughton, George, 121, 124
Bower Meadow, The, (Rossetti), 33½ x 26½, oil on canvas, *69*
Boxall, Sir William, 18, 87
Broken Vows (Calderon), 36 x 26¾, oil on canvas, *54*
Brown, Ford Madox, *Work*, *74-75*
Bubbles, painting by Millais, 65
Burlington Fine Arts Club, 84
Burne-Jones, Lady, 121
Burne-Jones, Sir Edward Coley, 105, 111, 124, 125, 128; painting by, *72*
Butterfly insignia, 80-81, 102, 112, *113*, 118, *128*, 141
By the Balcony, 8½ x 5½, lithograph, *166*, 174

Calderon, Philip Hermogenes, 55; *Broken Vows*, *54*
Cameron, Charles, 17
Campbell, Lady Archibald, 146-147
Caprice in Purple and Gold No. 2: The Golden Screen, 19¾ x 27, 79-80, *92-93*
Caricatures: drawings by Whistler, 20; Whistler a subject of, *8*, *9*, *24*, 124
Carlyle, Thomas, 74, 101, 102, 171; in paintings, *74-75*, *115*
Carpenter's Shop, The. See Christ in the House of His Parents
Carroll, Lewis, 66-67
Carte, Mrs. Richard D'Oyly, 149
Castagnary, Jules-Antoine, 46
Chelsea. See Nocturne in Blue and Green
Chelsea district, London, 66; in *Chelsea Shops*, 180, *181*; Cremorne Gardens in, 110, 111, 125-126; death of Whistler, 175; Howell's popularity in, 67; Nocturnes by Whistler depicting, 109-110, *138-139*; small oils by Whistler of, 171; Whistler's life and work in, 61, 66-67, 77-78, 78-79, 146, 180; White House, Whistler's residence in, *122*, 123, *130*
Chelsea Shops, 5¼ x 9¼, oil on wood panel, 180, *181*
Chelsea Snow. See Nocturne in Grey and Gold
Chinese art, 79, *81*, 88, 92, *148*
Christ in the House of His Parents (The Carpenter's Shop), (Millais), 34 x 55, oil on canvas, 64, *70-71*
Cigar-box label depicting Whistler (artist unknown), 4½ x 5½, chromo-lithograph, *175*
Classical art, 86, 88, 96, 97
Coast of Brittany, The, 42, 44
Coast Survey, United States, 21-22
Collins, Wilkie, 45
Collinson, James, 63
Converted British Family Sheltering a Christian Missionary from the Persecution of the Druids, A, (Hunt), 64
Corder, Rosa, 103
Courbet, Gustave, 22-23, 25-26, 33, 42, 81-82, 88; *Stormy Sea*, *33*
Cremorne Gardens, 110, 111, 125-126, 134

Dancing Faun, The, (Beardsley), 7⅛ x $4\frac{7}{16}$, pen and ink, *9*
Daubigny, François, 81
Daughter of Eve, 175
Debussy, Claude, 111, 173
Degas, Edgar, 147; *Bellelli Family, The*, *30*
Déjeuner sur l'herbe (Manet), 46, 47
Delacroix, Eugène, 22, 23, 47
Delannoy, Ernest, 24, 38
Delâtre, Auguste, 24
Derby Day, The, (Frith), 40 x 88, oil on canvas, 44, detail *49*, *50-51*
Dickens, Charles, 64
Disraeli, Benjamin, 123
Dodgson, Reverend Charles. *See* Carroll, Lewis
Dorsetshire Landscape, 12⅝ x 24¾, oil on canvas, *182-183*
du Maurier, George, 24, 39, 43, 124, 148, 173; works by, *24*, *43*, *44*, *148*
Dunn, Henry, *67*
Duret, Théodore, 147, *179*
Duveneck, Frank, 143

Eastern art. *See* Oriental art
Ecce Ancilla Domini (Rossetti), 64
Eden, Sir William and Lady, 172
Egg, Augustus Leopold, 44; *Past and Present, I, II and III*, *52*
Embroidered Curtain, The, $9\frac{7}{16}$ x $6\frac{5}{16}$, etching, *163*
English art: Academicians and, 61; character of, in Victorian period, 48, 52-53, 54-55, 56; Estheticism in, 147; French art versus, 62; Pre-Raphaelite movement in, 61, 62-65, 68, *69-75*; Whistler's influence on, 175
Estheticism, 147-148
Etching, 12, 24, 123, 131, 141-143, 145-146, 150, 171; needle, *40*. *See also* Whistler—etchings
Eugénie, French empress, 22
Exposition Universelle, Paris, 1855, 22

Falling Rocket, The. See Nocturne in Black and Gold
Fantin-Latour, Henri, 25, 26, 38, 43, 47, 67, 82, 174; sketch of, *27*; *Two Sisters*, *30*
Fantin-Latour in Bed, 9⅝ x 6½, chalk drawing, *27*
Far Eastern Art. *See* Oriental art
Fat Woman, The, (Beardsley), 7 x 6⅜, pen-and-ink drawing, *173*
Ferdinand Lured by Ariel (Millais), 63-64
Fine Art Society, London, 131, 141, 142, 145
Five Studies of Whistler (Menpes), 6⅞ x $5\frac{15}{16}$, dry point, *6*
Flaming June (Leighton), 46 x 46, oil on canvas, *56*
Ford, Sheridan, 170
Fors Clavigera, London magazine, 111, 121, 123

France: early sojourn of Whistler in Paris, 22-25; success and honors won by Whistler in, 171; Whistler's travel with Jo in, 42-43

Franklin, Maud, 103, 124, 125, 142, 145, 170; paintings of, *100, 137*

Freer, Charles, 118, 174, 176, *177,* 182-183

French art: "Art for Art's Sake" movement in, 45, 46; atelier system, 23; English art versus, 62; exhibitions at 1855 Exposition Universelle, 22-23; mood near turn of 19th Century, 173; realism in, 42

French Set, The, 24, 42, 143

Frick, Henry C., 174

Frith, William Powell, 44, 51, 61, 125, 128, 129; *Derby Day, The, 49, 50-51*

Fumette, 23-24, *28*

Fumette, Standing, 13⅝ x 8½, dry point, *28*

Fur Jacket, The. See Arrangement in Black and Brown

G*aiety Stage Door, The,* lithograph, 124

Gaiety Theatre, London, 124

Gautier, Théophile, 25, 43, 45

Gentle Art of Making Enemies, The, 170

Germ, The, 64

Gilbert and Sullivan, 148; versus by, *148, 149*

Gin Lane (Hogarth), engraving, 17

Girl with Fan (artist unknown), 9¼ high, terra cotta, *97*

Girlhood of Mary Virgin, The, (Rossetti), 32¾ x 25¾, oil on canvas, 63, *70*

Gleyre, Charles, 23

Godwin, Beatrix (Trixie). *See* Whistler, Beatrix (Trixie) Godwin

Godwin, Edward W., 169; house designed by, *122,* 123

Gold Scab—Eruption in FRiLthy Lucre, 73 x 55, oil on canvas, *131*

Golden Screen, The. See Caprice in Purple and Gold No. 2

Goupil Gallery, 172

Graves, Henry, 123

Gray, Euphemia, 121

Greaves, Walter and Harry, 106, 110; sketch by Walter, *108*

Gretchen at Heidelberg, etching, 24

Grey and Silver: The Angry Sea, 4⅞ x 8½, oil on wood panel, *180-181*

Grist, Mr., 142

Grosvenor Gallery, London, 111, 124, 125, 132, 138, 148

H*aden, Annie,* 25, 37, 41; in works, *29, 30-31,* 151

Haden, Deborah Whistler, 14, 16-18, 25, 37-39, 40-41, 84, 174; in works, *29, 30-31*

Haden, Dr. Seymour, 18, 37-40, 83-84

Harmony in Blue and Gold: The Peacock Room, 13′ 11⅞″ high, 33′ 2″ long, 19′ 11½″ wide, oil color and gold on leather and wood, 106-107, *118-119*

Harmony in Blue and Silver: Trouville, 81

Harmony in Flesh Color and Pink: Valérie, Lady Meux. See Valérie, Lady Meux

Harmony in Green and Rose: The Music Room, 37⅝ x 27⅞, oil on canvas, *29,* 40-41

Harmony in Grey and Green: Miss Cicely Alexander, 74¾ x 38½, oil on canvas, 102-103, 112, *113*

Harmony in Red: Lamplight, 169-170

Harnessed Samovar, The, (artist unknown), poster, 9⅜ x 15¼, *15*

Head of an Old Man Smoking, The, 25, 42

Heffernan, Jo, 33, 40-43, 79, 81, 83, 92, 103; in works, *34-35, 42, 60, 89-91, 93*

Hogarth, William, 17, 44

Howell, Charles Augustus, 67, 121, 122, 123, 130, 131; sketch of, *67*

Howells, William Dean, 172

Hunt, William Holman, 62-65, 68, 70-72, 111; works by, *62, 70, 73*

Huth, Louis, 130

I*dle and the Industrious Apprentice, The,* (du Maurier), cartoon, *24*

Impressionism, 11, 125

Ingres, Jean-Auguste-Dominique, 22, 23, 82

Interior decoration, 78, *104, 105,* 106-107, *118-119, 169*

International Exposition of 1887, Paris, 171

Ionides, Alexander, 42, 43

Ionides, Helen, 82

Ionides, Luke, 42

Irving, Sir Henry, *136,* 137

Israel in Egypt (Poynter), 54 x 125, oil on canvas, *58-59*

J*ames, Henry,* 124-125, 129-130, 175

Japanese art, 79, 80, 86, 92-93, *94*

Jeckyll, Henry, 105-106

Jo, La Belle Irlandaise (Courbet), 42

K*'ang Hsi plates, 81*

Kitchen, The, 8⅞ x 6⅛, etching, *154*

Kiyonaga, Torii, *94*

L*a Touche, Rose,* 121

Lady Meux Triplex, 4¾ x 7¾, drawing with watercolor, *146*

Lady of Shalott, The, (Hunt), 74 x 57½, oil on canvas, 72, *73*

Lamplight. See Harmony in Red

Lange Lijzen of the Six Marks, The. See Purple and Rose: The Lange Lijzen of the Six Marks

Last Day in the Old Home, The, (Martineau), 42¼ x 57, oil on canvas, *52-53*

Last Evening, The, (Tissot), 28½ x 40½, oil on canvas, *55*

Legros, Alphonse, 25, 33, *34-35,* 38, 42

Leighton, Sir Frederick, 85; *Flaming June,* 56

Leyland, Frederick, 77, 104-107, *116, 131,* 172, 178

Leyland, Mrs. Frederick, 103-104, 116, *117,* 178

Lime-burner, The, 9⅞ x 6⅞, etching, *155*

Lindsay, Sir Coutts, 111

Lithography, 123-124, 173

Little White Girl, The. See Symphony in White No. 2

London: early artistic life of Whistler in, 26, 37-39; etchings of, in "The Thames Set," 150; Grosvenor Gallery exhibitions, 111, 124-125

Long House—Dyer's—Amsterdam, The, 6½ x 10⁹/₁₆, etching, *164-165*

Lorenzo and Isabella (Millais), 63

Lowell, Mass., *Whistler's Birthplace* (Pratt), 6 x 7¾, etching, 11, *12,* 14

M*aclise, Daniel,* 61

McNeill, Anna. *See* Whistler, Anna McNeill

McNeill, William, 13

Mallarmé Stéphane, 173

Manet, Édouard, *Déjeuner sur l'herbe,* 46, 47

Mantz, Paul, 47

Marriage à la Mode (Hogarth), engraving, *17*

Martineau, Robert Braithwaite, *Last Day in the Old Home, The,* *52-53*

Mary Virgin (Rossetti), 63

Mast, The, 13⅜ x 6⁷/₁₆, etching, 143, *158*

Maurice, F. D., in Ford's *Work,* 74-75

Menpes, Mortimer, 6, 11, 174

Mère Gérard, La, 25, 42

Meredith, George, 66

Meux, Lady Valérie, 146-147, *178*

Millais, John Everett, 39, 62-65, 68, 111, 121, 145; painting by, *70-71*

Miss Cicely Alexander. See Harmony in Grey and Green

Mrs. Frederick R. Leyland, 77⅛ x 40¼, oil on canvas, 103-104, 116, *117,* 178

Monet, Claude, 81, 169

Montesquiou, Count Robert de, 171

Moore, Albert Joseph, 85-86, 88, 125, 128

Morris, William, 65, 105; designs by, *64, 65*

Morris chair, *65*

Mother. See Arrangement in Grey and Black No. 1: The Artist's Mother

Murger, Henri, 22

Music Room, The, etching, 40

Music Room, The, painting. *See*

Harmony in Green and Rose: The Music Room

N*ankin pottery collection, 81,* 124

Napoleon III, 22, 46, 47

Nation, The, 124, 129

Nature versus art, 62, 68, 149, 167-168

Needle, etching, photograph of, actual size 3¼, *40*

Neoclassicism, 23, 85

New York City, N.Y.: *Mother* in, 145; *Patience* in, 148

Newton, Kathleen, 55

Nicholas I, Russian czar, 14-15, 16

No Walk Today (Anderson), 19¾ x 15¾, oil on canvas, *36*

Nocturne in Black and Gold: The Falling Rocket, 23¾ x 18¾, oil on panel, 109, 132, *133, 134;* Ruskin on, 111, 121, 122-123; at Whistler-Ruskin trial, 125-126, 127, 128; Wilde on, 148

Nocturne in Blue and Gold: Old Battersea Bridge, 26¾ x 20, oil on canvas, 134, *135;* at Ruskin trial, 126, 128

Nocturne in Blue and Gold: Valparaiso, 29¾ x 19¾, oil on canvas, *76*

Nocturne in Blue and Green: Chelsea, 14⅞ x 18, oil on panel, *138-139*

Nocturne in Blue and Silver, 109

Nocturne in Grey and Gold: Chelsea Snow, 110

Nocturnes, 47; character and mood of, 12, 17, 138; meaning of and comments on, 109-111, 125-127

Note in Red, A, 5¼ x 9¼, oil on wood panel, *180*

O*ld Battersea Bridge. See Nocturne in Blue and Gold*

Old Putney Bridge, 7⅞ x 11¾, etching, *front end paper*

On the Brain—Mr. Whistler (May), caricature, *128*

On Post in Camp, 4 pen sketches, 9½ x 8 (each), *18*

Oriental art: collection by Whistler of, 78-79, 88, *94,* 148; elements of, in Whistler's "ideal style" period, 86; Freer's and Whistler's appreciation of, 183; influence on Whistler, 79-80, *81,* 88, *89-91;* Kiyonaga's woodcuts, *94;* Nocturnes influenced by, 110; popularity of, *81*

P*age, "News from Nowhere"* (Morris), type face, 64

Painting techniques, 43, 82, 102-103, 110, 141, 144, 147

Palaces, The, 9⅞ x 14⅛, etching, *160-161*

Palmer, Mrs. George, 14

Pancake recipe, *106*

Paris, 11, 22-25, 26, 42, 46-47, 83-84, 172, 173

Past and Present I, II and III (Egg), each 25 x 30, oil on canvas, 44, *52*

Pastel painting, 144, 145
Pater, Walter, 147
Patience, operetta (Gilbert and Sullivan), *148, 149*
Peacock Room. See Harmony in Blue and Gold
Peacock Room episode, 106-107, *118-119*
Peacock Room Middle Panel, preliminary sketch, *104*
Peacock Room Shutter Panels, preliminary sketches, *105*
Peasant Woman, etching, 24
Pennell, Joseph and Elizabeth, 93, 174
Pennsylvania Academy of Fine Arts, Philadelphia, 145
"Personae," by Pound, 185
Peter the Great, Russian czar, 16, 17
Philip, John Birnie, 169
Piccadilly, London magazine, 123
Pissarro, Camille, 171
Plein air painting, 43
Poetry: Mallarmé's approach to, 173; Whistler's turn toward, 12
Portrait of Charles L. Freer, $20\frac{3}{8}$ x $12\frac{1}{2}$, oil on wood panel, *177*
Portrait of Dante Gabriel Rossetti (Hunt), $11\frac{7}{8}$ x 9, oil on canvas, *62*
Portrait of Major Whistler, 12 x $9\frac{7}{8}$, oil on wood panel, *13*
Portrait of Théodore Duret. See Arrangement in Flesh Color and Black
Portrait of Whistler (Way), $5\frac{3}{8}$ x $3\frac{3}{4}$, lithograph, *7*
Portrait painting: goals of Whistler in, 112; late work by Whistler in, 146-147, 171; Whistler's habit of naming portraits Arrangements or Harmonies, 12; Whistler's success in, 101-104
Poster and Redraft for sale of White House, 130
Pound, Ezra, *185*
Poynter, Sir Edward John, *7, 24*, 44, 85; *Israel in Egypt, 58-59*
Pre-Raphaelites, 61, 62-65, 68, *69-75;* concepts of, spread by Morris' designs, *64;* loss of prestige of, 147; realism and, 68, 70; restoration of Leyland's house and, 105; Ruskin's support of, 64; theories on art, 68; Whistler and, 11, 88
Princess Victoria of Wales in her boudoir (artist unknown), drawn from a photograph, 78
Princesse du Pays de la Porcelaine, La, $78\frac{3}{4}$ x $45\frac{3}{4}$, oil on canvas, 80, 105, 106, 107, 116, *118*, 172
Prinsep, Val, 24, 109
Punch, London magazine, 24, *44*, 124, *129*, 148
Purple and Rose: The Lange Lijzen of the Six Marks, 36 x 24, oil on canvas, 79, *93*

Quilter, Harry, 131, 146

Raphael, 62
Realism: in Courbet's art, 23, 33; in French art and in Whistler's early works, 11, 25, 42; influence of Courbet's realism on Whistler, 26, 33, 42, 88; Poynter and, 58-59; Pre-Raphaelites' art theories and, 68, 70; Whistler's revolt against, 12, 42, 82, 85
Reed, Edward Tennyson, 9
Religious themes, 65, 70
Rienzi (Hunt), 63
Riva No. 2, The, $8\frac{1}{2}$ x 12, etching, *back end paper*
Rodin, Auguste, 174
Romanticism: influence of Pre-Raphaelites on, 88; in Victorian period, 48, 52-53, 54–55
Rose and Silver: The Princess from the Land of Porcelaine. See Princesse du Pays de la Porcelaine, La
Rossetti, Christina, 64-65
Rossetti, Dante Gabriel, 61-68, 80, 83, 91, 111; photograph of, *66;* poem by, *62;* portrait of, *62;* works, by, *69, 70*
Rossetti, William, 63, 66
Rotherhithe, etching, 44
Royal Academy, London: *At the Piano* exhibited at the, 25, 39; attitude of Whistler toward, 11-12; *Coast of Brittany* and *Thames in Ice* at 1862 show, 42, 44; Frith's *Derby Day* at the, 51; Millais elected Associate of the, 65; position of, in English art, 61; Pre-Raphaelite movement as protest against, 62; Pre-Raphaelites' works accepted by the, 63-64; storeroom, *86; Symphony in White No. 1*, rejection by, 44; *Symphony in White No. 2* exhibited at the, 79; Whistler's portrait by Boxall at the, 18; Whistler's portrait of his mother exhibited at the, 87
Royal Academy—the Hurly Burly (artist unknown), oil on canvas, *86*
Royal Academy Students' Club, 169
Ruskin, John, 64, 67, 111, 121-123, 125-130, 132, 134, 136, 138; cartoons of, *128, 129;* photograph of, *66*
Russia: cartoon depicting new railroad, *15;* soldiers sketched by Whistler, *16;* Whistler's youth in, 14-18
Russian Dragoons, sketch, *16*

St. Petersburg, Russia, Whistler's youth spent in, 14-18
Salon des Refusés, Paris, 46, 47
Salon of 1859, 25
Salon of 1863, 46
Sargent, John Singer, 144, 172
Scapegoat, The, (Hunt), 34 x 55, oil on canvas, *70*, 71
Scottish Royal Academy, 16
Seascapes, 33, 42
Self-Portrait, c. 1900, $24\frac{1}{2}$ x $18\frac{1}{4}$, oil on canvas, *184*
Seton, Dorothy, 175
Seurat, Georges, 111
Shaw, Norman, 105
Sickert, Walter, 147, 169, 174
Siddal, Elizabeth, 65, 66, 68; poem on, *62*
Sir Henry Irving. See Arrangement in Black No. 3
Six Projects, sketches, 86
Six-Mark Teapot, The, (du Maurier), cartoon, *148*
Sketch of C. A. Howell (Dunn), pen and ink, *67*
Smithy, The, $6\frac{7}{8}$ x 9, etching and dry point, *162*
Snowstorm (Turner), 128
Society of British Artists, 169, 170
Society of British Artists Exhibition, 7 x 6, pen-and-ink sketch, *169*
"Society of Three," 25
Solomon, Simeon, 66
Soup à Trois Sous, etching, 40
Spartali, Christine, 80
Spartali, Michael, 77, 80
Stephens, Frederick George, 63
Stormy Sea (Courbet), $46\frac{3}{16}$ x $62\frac{15}{16}$, oil on canvas, *33*
Stott, William, 170
"Sudden Light," poem (Rossetti), *62*
Sullivan, Sir Arthur, 148
Survey Plate, engraving, *21*
Swinburne, Algernon Charles, 66, 67, 77-79, *80*, 81, 91
Symphony, A, (Ward), $12\frac{1}{4}$ x $7\frac{1}{4}$, colored lithograph, *8*
Symphony in White No. 1: The White Girl, $84\frac{1}{2}$ x $42\frac{1}{2}$, oil on canvas, 42-43, *60*
Symphony in White No. 2: The Little White Girl, $30\frac{1}{8}$ x $20\frac{1}{8}$, oil on canvas, 79, *80, 89-91*
Symphony in White No. 3, $20\frac{1}{4}$ x $30\frac{1}{8}$, oil on canvas, 86, 97, *98-99*

"*Tableaux vivants*," 61
Tanagra figurines, 88; *Girl with Fan, 97*
Taylor, Tom, 125, 128
"Ten O'Clock, The," 149, 167-168
Tennyson, Alfred Lord, 72
Thames in Ice, The, $29\frac{3}{8}$ x $21\frac{3}{4}$, oil on canvas, *32*, 44
Thames River, 33, 37-38, 44, 67; in works, *32, 34-35, 108, 155, 156-157*
"Thames Set, The," etchings, 150
Thomas, Sergeant, 37, 40, 42
Thomas Carlyle. See Arrangement in Grey and Black No. 2
Thompson, Joseph, 38
Thumping Legacy, The, (du Maurier), program for play, *43*
Times, The, London newspaper, 64
Tissot, James (Jacques) Joseph, 54-55; *Last Evening, The, 55*
Traghetto No. 2, The, $9\frac{9}{16}$ x $11\frac{15}{16}$, etching, 143, *158-159*
Trilby, by du Maurier, 24, 173
Trouville. See Harmony in Blue and Silver
Turner, J. M. W., 110, 128
Twain, Mark, 12, 108
Twelve Months in the South (Kiyonaga), wood-block prints; "Fourth Month" $19\frac{7}{8}$ x $14\frac{5}{8}$, "Sixth Month" $15\frac{3}{4}$ x $10\frac{3}{4}$, *94*
Two Brothers, The, (artist unknown), miniature, *14*
Two Sisters, The, (Fantin-Latour), $38\frac{9}{16}$ x $51\frac{3}{16}$, oil on canvas, *30*

United States Coast Survey, 21
United States Military Academy Song of the Graduates, $13\frac{3}{8}$ x $10\frac{1}{4}$, lithograph, *19*

Valérie, Lady Meux, $76\frac{1}{4}$ x $36\frac{5}{8}$, oil on canvas, 146, *178*
Valparaiso. See Nocturne in Blue and Gold
Variations in Blue and Green, $18\frac{1}{4}$ x $24\frac{5}{8}$, oil on prepared Academy Board mounted on panel, *96-97*
Variations in Flesh Color and Green: The Balcony, $24\frac{1}{4}$ x $14\frac{1}{4}$, oil on wood panel, *94*
Venice, Italy, 131, 141, 142, 143-144, 146, 150; Whistler's works in, *140, 158, 159, 160-161*
Victoria, Queen, 22, 48, 169
Victorian period: art concepts of, 126; artists and, 38; Esthetic Movement and, 147; Frith's depiction of, 44; interior decoration during, store advertisement of, *78;* Romanticism and subjects popular in art of, 48, 52-53, 54-55, 56; Whistler's attitude toward, 9
Voices in the Night (artist unknown), caricature, $3\frac{1}{4}$ x $6\frac{3}{8}$, *129*

Wales, Prince of, 146
Wapping, London area, 37-38, 40
Wapping on Thames, 28 x 40, oil on canvas, *34-35*, 40
Ward, Leslie, *A Symphony, 8*
Watts, George, 101
Way, Thomas, 123, 131; lithograph of Whistler, *7*
Weary, $7\frac{3}{4}$ x $5\frac{1}{8}$, etching, *42*
Webb, Philip, *65*
Webster, Daniel, 19
West Point, 13, 18, 19, 20
Whistler, Anna Mathilda, 12, 14, 15-19, 77, 78, 86, 87, 104, 145, 146, 171; photograph of, *13*, portrait of, *114*
Whistler, Beatrix (Trixie) Godwin, *166*, 169, 170, *173*, 174
Whistler, Charles, 14
Whistler, Deborah. *See* Haden, Deborah Whistler
Whistler, Dr. Daniel, 13
Whistler, Dr. William, *14*, 16, 18, 77, 81, *82*, 130, 145, 174
Whistler, George, 14, 19, 22
Whistler, George Washington, 13-15, 18; portrait of, *13*
Whistler, James McNeill, 11; and abstract art, 12, 42, 85, 175; "Address" to Queen Victoria, 169: analysis of influences on, 42, 86, 88, 92, 94, 97; apprenticeship in Paris, 11, 22-25; art, theories on, 8, 12, 43, 84-85, 125-127, 149; art

collection by, 78-79, 88, 148; assessment of work, 174-175; birth, 11, *12*, 14; Boxall's portrait of, 18; butterfly insignia, 80-81, 141; and Carlyle, 101-102; in cartoons on trial, *128, 129*; changes in art of, 11, 12, 82, 86; and Chelsea, 61, 66-67, 77-78, 78-79, 146, 180; with the Coast Survey, 21-22; and Courbet, 25, 26, 42, 81-82; death of, 175; death of mother, 145; drawing for sheet music, *19*; and du Maurier, *24*, 39, *44*; education of, 16-17, 19, 23; Esthetic Movement and, 147; etching technique, 12, 24, 143, 150; explanation of his work at Ruskin trial, 125-130, 134; and Fantin-Latour, 25, 26, 38, 43, 47, 67, 82; financial situation and bankruptcy, 123, 130-131, 172; and Franklin, Maud, 103, 142, 145, 170; and Freer, 176, 182-183; and Fumette, 23-24; *Gentle Art of Making Enemies* published by, 170; health of, 18, 175; and Heffernan, Jo, 41-42, 42-43, 79, 81, 83, 103; "ideal style" period, 85; illegitimate children of, 41, 145; incidents of violence, 83-84; and Leyland, Mrs., 103-104; libel suit against Ruskin, 111, 121, 122-123, 125-130, 134, 136, 138; lithography, 123-124; marriage, 166, 169-170, 173-174; miniature with brother, *14*; and mother, 15-16, 77-78; Nocturnes, meaning of, and reaction to, 109-111; Oriental art and, 79-80, 86, 88, 110; painting techniques, 43, 82, 102-103, 110, 141, 147; pastels of Venice, 141, 144; Peacock Room episode, 106-107, 118; personality and behavior of, 7, 8, 11-12, 16, 20, 39-40, 41, 84, 102, 107-109, 131, 141, 142, 175; photograph near etching press, *142*; physical appearance, *6-10*, 108-109; popularity of portrait of mother, 12, *114*; portrait painting, 101-104, 146-147; portraits and caricatures of, *6-10*; Pound's poem to, 185; prestige and success, 168-169, 172, 174; Royal Academy, exhibition of works at the, 25, 39, 42, 44, 79, 87; St. Petersburg, life in, 14-18; self-portraits by, *95, 120, 184*; small oils painted late in life, 171; Society of British Artists, presidency of, 169; South America, 82-83; table

palette of, *40*; "Ten O'Clock" lecture, 167-168; and Thames River, 37-38, *152, 155, 156-157*; theater, interest in, 124; titles given to his works, 12, 47, 85; trips to France with Jo Heffernan, 42-43, 81-82; voyage to Italy and sojourn in Venice, 131, 141-144; West Point, 20-21; White House, *122*; and Wilde, 148, 149

Whistler—drawings: Aunt Alicia, 16; cadets at West Point, 18; caricatures at West Point, 20; cartoon on himself, *146*; for catalogue illustrating art collection, watercolor, *81*, 124; cover for sheet music at West Point, *19*; *Fantin-Latour in Bed*, *27*; *Head of an Old Man Smoking, The*, 25, 42; preliminary sketches for dining room of Leylands' town house, *104, 105*; of Russian soldiers, *16*

Whistler—etchings and dry points: *Annie Haden*, 151; *Axenfeld*, 153; *Becquet*, 152; *Black Lion Wharf*, 156-157; Boston harbor, *21*; *Embroidered Curtain, The*, 163; *French Set, The*, 24, 42, 143; *Fumette, Standing*, 28; *Gretchen at Heidelberg*, 24; *Kitchen, The*, 154; *Lime-burner, The*, 155; *Long House —Dyer's—Amsterdam, The*, 164-165; *Mast, The*, 143, 158; *Music Room, The*, 40; *Old Putney Bridge*, front end paper; *Palaces, The*, 160-161; *Peasant Woman*, 24; *The Riva No. 2*, back end paper; *Rotherhithe*, 44; *Smithy, The*, 162; *Soup à Trois Sous*, 40; *Traghetto No. 2, The*, 143, 158-159; *Weary*, 42

Whistler—miscellany: *Alley in Venice*, pastel, *140*, 144; *By the Balcony*, *166*, 174; *Gaiety Stage Door, The*, 124; of Howells, 172; Paris, views of, 173

Whistler—paintings: *Arrangement in Black and Brown: The Fur Jacket*, 137; *Arrangement in Black and White No. 1: The Young American*, 100, 124, 125; *Arrangement in Black No. 3: Sir Henry Irving*, 136, 137; *Arrangement in Black: Portrait of F. R. Leyland*, *116*, 178; *Arrangement in Flesh Color and Black: Portrait of Théodore Duret*, 147, *179*; *Arrangement in Grey and Black

No. 1: The Artist's Mother*, 12, 86-87, *114*, 145-146, 171; *Arrangement in Grey and Black No. 2: Thomas Carlyle*, 101-102, *115*, 171; *Arrangement in Grey: Self-Portrait*, 120; *Arrangement in White and Black*, 146; *Artist in His Studio, The*, 94, *95*; *Artist's Mother, The. See Arrangement in Grey and Black No. 1*; *At the Piano*, 25, *30-31*, 38-39, 42; *Blue Wave: Biarritz, The*, 33, 43; Campbell, Lady Archibald, portrait of, 146-147; *Caprice in Purple and Gold No. 2: The Golden Screen*, 79-80, *92-93*; *Chelsea Shops*, 180, *181*; *Coast of Brittany, The*, 42, 44; Corder, Rosa, portrait of, 103; *Daughter of Eve*, 175; *Dorsetshire Landscape*, *182-183*; Eden, Lady, portrait of, 172; *Gold Scab—Eruption in FRiLthy Lucre*, 131; *Grey and Silver: The Angry Sea*, 180-181; *Harmony in Blue and Gold: The Peacock Room*, 106-107, 118-119; *Harmony in Blue and Silver: Trouville*, 81; *Harmony in Flesh Color and Pink: Valérie, Lady Meux*, 146, *178*; *Harmony in Green and Rose: The Music Room*, 29, *40-41*; *Harmony in Grey and Green: Miss Cicely Alexander*, 102-103, 112, *113*; *Harmony in Red: Lamplight*, 169-170; *Mère Gérard, La*, 25, 42; Montesquiou, Count Robert de, portrait of, 171; *Mother. See Arrangement in Grey and Black No. 1: The Artist's Mother*; *Mrs. Frederick R. Leyland*, 103-104, 116, *117*; *Nocturne in Black and Gold: The Falling Rocket*, 111, 121, 122-123, 125-126, 127, 128, 132, *133, 134*; *Nocturne in Blue and Gold: Old Battersea Bridge*, 126, 128, 134, *135*; *Nocturne in Blue and Gold: Valparaiso*, 76; *Nocturne in Blue and Green: Chelsea*, 138-139; *Nocturne in Blue and Silver*, 109; *Nocturne in Grey and Gold: Chelsea Snow*, 110; *Note in Red, A*, *180*; *Portrait of Charles L. Freer*, *177*; *Princesse du Pays de la Porcelaine, La*, 80, 105, 106, 107, 116, *118*, 172; *Purple and Rose: The Lange Lijzen of the Six Marks*, 79, *93*; *Self-Portrait*, c. 1900, *184*; *Symphony in White No. 1: The White Girl*,

42-43, 44-45, 46, 47, *60*; *Symphony in White No. 2: The Little White Girl*, 79, *89-91*; *Symphony in White No. 3*, 86, 97, *98-99*; *Thames in Ice, The*, 32, 44; *Valérie, Lady Meux*, 146, *178*; *Variations in Blue and Green*, *96-97*; *Variations in Flesh Color and Green: The Balcony*, 94; *Wapping on Thames*, 34-35, 40

Whistler, John, 13
Whistler, Mary Swift, 13, 14
Whistler As the Letter "Q" (du Maurier), initial design, *44*
Whistler Giving Evidence in the Case of Pennell v. "The Saturday Review" and Another (Beerbohm), 12 x 10¾, pen, ink and color wash, *8*
Whistler and His Printing Press (Dornac), 10 x 8, photograph, *142*
Whistler Laughing (Menpes), 7½ x 5½, dry point, *10*
Whistler in Paris (Poynter), 6 x 6, pencil drawing, *7*
Whistler Rowing on the Thames (Greaves), 9 x 11¼ pen-and-ink sketch, *108*
Whistler-Ruskin trial, 111, 121, 122-123, 125-130, 134, 136, 138; cartoons of, *128, 129*
Whistler on the Stairs of the Beefsteak Club (Reed), 6½ x 5½, pencil drawing, *9*
Whistler's Mother. See Arrangement in Grey and Black No. 1
Whistler's Mother, painting by Whistler. *See Arrangement in Grey and Black No. 1*
White Girl, The. See Symphony in White No. 1: The White Girl
White House, *122*, 123, 131
Wilde, Oscar, 148, 149
Williams, "Stonington Bill," 25
Wills, William Gorman, 128
"Winged Victory" (Rodin), sculpture, *174*
Woman in White, 45
Woods, Henry, 144
Woolner, Thomas, 63
Work (Brown), 53 x 77⅛, oil on canvas, 74-75
World's Columbian Exposition of 1893, Chicago, 150

Young American, The. See *Arrangement in Black and White No. 1*

Zola, Émile, 46

The text for this book was set in Bodoni Book, a typeface that was named for its Italian designer, Giambattista Bodoni (1740-1813). One of the earliest modern typefaces, Bodoni Book differs from more evenly weighted old-style characters in the greater contrast between thick and thin parts of letters. The Bodoni character is vertical with a thin, straight serif.

xxx